"Piper has done it again. His outstanding book *Think* promises to shepherd a generation about the Christian commitment to the life of the mind. Deeply biblical and uniquely balanced, *Think* practices what it preaches: it is an accessible, intellectually rich study that calls the reader to renewed love for God and others."

J. P. Moreland, distinguished professor of philosophy, Biola University

"John Piper offers much wise advice on the importance of Christian thinking as a way of loving God with our minds and as part of delighting in God above all things."

George Marsden, emeritus professor of history, University of Notre Dame; author, *Jonathan Edwards: A Life*

"Do you ever wish you could feel more deeply about things you know are true? Has it been a while since you were moved to tears at the thought of Christ's death for your sins? It's not mysterious: those who *feel deeply* about the gospel are those who *think deeply* about the gospel. In these pages John Piper will convince you that thinking is the sturdy foundation for our easily misguided affections. If you want to feel profoundly, learn to think carefully. And start by reading this book!"

C. J. Mahaney, senior pastor, Sovereign Grace Church of Louisville

"An essential dimension of Christian discipleship is the life of the mind, and this may well be the most neglected Christian responsibility of our times. God has made us intelligible creatures, and he has given us the stewardship of intellectual faculties that should drive us to think in ways that bring him greatest glory. In this new book, John Piper provides brilliant analysis, warm encouragement, and a faithful model of Christian thinking. This book is a primer for Christian thinking that is urgently needed in our time."

R. Albert Mohler Jr., president, Southern Baptist Theological Seminary

"The book provides an excellent, robust biblical foundation for thinking in service of the glory of Christ. It challenges human attitudes and provides sound responses to the temptations either to reject vigorous thinking as unspiritual, to pursue "neutral" scholarship, or to take pride in thinking and fall into autonomy."

Vern Poythress, professor, New Testament interpretation, Westminster Theological Seminary

"Thinking—the alert, meticulous, probing, logical, critical use of the mind—will be a highway either to godliness or to its opposite, depending on how it is done. Taking leads from Jonathan Edwards, John Piper surefootedly plots the true path here. His book should be, and I hope will be, widely read."

J. I. Packer, Board of Governors' Professor of Theology, Regent College

"We cannot feel like Christians or act like Christians if we don't think like Christians. As his writing and preaching attest, John Piper is convinced that the heart cannot embrace that which the mind does not recognize as good, true, and beautiful. This wise book not only makes that point well, but does so by exhibiting in its style and grace the beauty of holy thoughts. This is a timely missive from a seasoned pastor."

Michael S. Horton, J. Gresham Machen Professor of Systematic Theology and Apologetics, Westminster Seminary California

"Those who are skittish when it comes to rigorous study, deep thinking, and theological precision have wanted us to believe that our problem is the mind, when in fact it's the flesh. The problem isn't knowledge, it's pride. John Piper reminds us in this excellent book that what we need isn't less thinking, but clearer, biblical, and more God-centered thinking. Reading and thinking about *Think* will set you on your way to the renewal of the mind that the Scriptures insist is the catalyst for heartfelt joy and growth in godliness. I highly recommend it!"

Sam Storms, pastor, Bridgeway Church, Oklahoma City, Oklahoma

"John Piper has written a wise and passionate book about the importance of loving God with our minds. After all, we are commanded to do so! But as Piper explains, Christians have not always been very attentive to that commandment. With clarity and directness, he reveals the obstacles that prevent us from using our minds as God intended—but also shows the delights and benefits of doing so. Especially for those who fear intellectualism, this book will be a bracing tonic, and an encouragement besides."

Alan Jacobs, distinguished professor of humanities in the honors program, Baylor University

"Some Christians don't think nearly enough; others are prone to think in the wrong way. I warmly commend John Piper's appeal to all believers to be diligent in engaging our minds and to do so with God-honoring humility and Christ-loving passion."

Vaughan Roberts, rector of St. Ebbe's, Oxford, England; director, The Proclamation Trust; author, *God's Big Picture*

"No one—in speaking, writing, or living—combines mind, heart, and faith more passionately than John Piper. It is our great good fortune that these are the direct topics of exploration in this book. As always with John, the result is insight, encouragement, and a call to action."

Daniel Taylor, author, *The Myth of Certainty*; *Tell Me a Story*; and *Death Comes for the Destructionist*

"*Think* is a bracing gust of fresh air in a stale and musty room that hasn't been aired out in a generation or more. In this book, the love of God and the life of the mind are passionately connected in the way the Scriptures require, and the result is a direct challenge to the intellectual sloppiness and disobedience that is so characteristic of our time."

Douglas Wilson, pastor, Christ Church, Moscow, Idaho

OTHER BOOKS BY JOHN PIPER:

The Pleasures of God

Desiring God

The Dangerous Duty of Delight

Finally Alive

Future Grace

A Hunger for God

Seeing and Savoring Jesus Christ

What's the Difference?

Don't Waste Your Life

When I Don't Desire God

Fifty Reasons Why Jesus Came to Die

God Is the Gospel

What Jesus Demands from the World

When the Darkness Will Not Lift

Spectacular Sins

John Calvin and His Passion for the Majesty of God

This Momentary Marriage

A Sweet and Bitter Providence

The Life
of the Mind
and the Love
of God

Think

JOHN PIPER

CROSSWAY®

WHEATON, ILLINOIS

Library of Congress Cataloging-in-Publication Data
Piper, John, 1946–
    Think: the life of the mind and the love of God / John Piper.
        p. cm.
    Includes index.
    ISBN 978-1-4335-2071-6 (hc) — ISBN 978-1-4335-2072-3 (pdf)
    ISBN 978-1-4335-2073-0 (mobipocket)
    ISBN 978-1-4335-2074-7 (ebk)
    1. Thought and thinking—Religious aspects—Christianity.
2. Learning and scholarship—Religious aspects—Christianity.
I. Title.
BV4598.4.P56   2010
230.01—dc22   2009051489

Crossway is a publishing ministry of Good News Publishers.

CH		28	27	26	25	24	23	22	21	20	19	18
15	14	13	12	11	10	9	8	7	6	5	4	3

To

Mark Noll and Nathan Hatch

Class of '68

Contents

Foreword

Among many important benefits from hearing or reading good sermons is the stimulus to think more clearly about God and his ways. When the sermons are about thinking itself, the stimulus is all the stronger.

John Piper's book on thinking is more sermon-like than an actual sermon. Yet because of how it engages the Scriptures and seeks to apply Scripture to real-life questions, the book functions like a good sermon. Its main texts are taken from Proverbs 2 and 2 Timothy 2, an Old Testament passage and a New Testament passage that both urge followers of God to think carefully. Insight and understanding are the goals in Proverbs 2; thinking over what Paul has said to Timothy is the purpose in view in the other passage.

As in good sermons, Piper wants to set these texts in their proper contexts, and this is where the payoff comes. Paul urges Timothy to think carefully, "for the Lord will give you understanding in everything" (2 Tim. 2:7). The author of Proverbs urges careful thought in order to find "silver" and "hidden treasure," which are then defined as "the fear of the Lord" and "the knowledge of God." With that relationship secured—between thinking and finding the knowledge of God—Piper can then develop his arguments that move from Scripture to real-life problems.

The real-life problems are two sides of the same coin. From the one side, spiritually minded people may conclude that since the Holy Spirit is the source of all life and truth, it is not important to work at thinking, reading, and learning. From the other side, intellectually minded people may conclude that since God wants us to think, read, and learn, these activities are supremely important in and of themselves.

Piper strikes hard at both those conclusions. He holds up instead the results of patient biblical exposition ranging through the Scriptures to underscore two alternative truths that speak directly to the contemporary situation. First, against anti-intellectual tendencies, he argues that careful thinking is integral to a full apprehension of the gospel.

Second, against the prideful use of the intellect, he argues that clear thinking following biblical patterns will lead away from self to a full delight in God's grace as the key to every aspect of existence.

Different readers will doubtless find different aspects of Piper's exposition most arresting, but I came away especially provoked to meditate by his efforts to fathom two passages, which I have also pondered. One is Luke 10:21, where Jesus says that God has "hidden these things from the wise and understanding and revealed them to little children." Piper's careful exegesis shows convincingly that Jesus' words are meant to promote humility in the use of all gifts, including intelligence, rather than to deny the intellect. The other passage is 1 Corinthians 1:20, where the apostle Paul says that God has "made foolish the wisdom of the world." Again, careful exegesis shows that the intent of the passage is to differentiate between wisdom used to exalt the creature and wisdom employed to honor the Creator. This conclusion is later summarized in one of Piper's many striking phrases: "The cross is the continental divide between human wisdom and divine wisdom."

The real-life payoff from carefully examining such passages could hardly be more timely. Much in contemporary American life promotes sloppy thinking or the use of careful thinking for human self-promotion. Much in conservative Christian churches promotes suspicion of modern learning or the use of reactionary emotion to replace thinking. Piper sets out the biblical alternative: thinking (as clearly as possible) linked *with* the affections (treasuring God as highest good); respect for the intellect *with* caution against intellectual pride; and commitment to diligent study *with* total reliance on God's grace. For believers, this is the way to go; for unbelievers, this is the way to life.

When the request came to prepare a short foreword for this book, I had to smile at the propitious timing of the Lord. Was it only a coincidence, I wondered, that I was being asked to read John Piper's book on the imperative of Christ-centered thinking in the very days when I was drafting the last words for my sequel to *The Scandal of the Evangelical Mind*, which was published some years ago? The chuckle came because, like John's volume, my book looks to John 1, Hebrews 1, and especially to Colossians 1 for what these passages say about "all things" being created in, by, through, and for Jesus Christ. I am also trying to show that careful study is a divinely ordained necessity, but one that should never replace a Christian's total reliance on God's grace. Like John, I am urging believers to be deadly serious about studying the word, but not at all serious about themselves.

My wife, Maggie, wondered if my book, which will be called *Jesus Christ and the Life of the Mind*, would suffer in competition with John's. I responded that there is enough difference to tell them apart. John's biblical exposition is much more extensive, and his exposition dramatizes more powerfully the proper role of hard human thinking in the enjoyment of Christ. My book says a few things about science (especially evolution) that many of John's appreciative readers, and maybe John himself, might not approve. And for my effort at promoting Christ-centered thinking, I make more use of some Catholic thinkers and of the great ancient statements of orthodox Christian faith (the Apostles' Creed, the Nicene Creed, and the Chalcedonian Definition of Christ's person).

Yet since the basic message of what I'm trying to say is exactly the same as what you will read in *Think: The Life of the Mind and the Love of God*, I am delighted to commend the book that lies before you and am completely unconcerned if this is the only book you read on this vitally important topic!

It has been my privilege to know John Piper since we were literature majors living in the same dorm at Wheaton College in what now seems close to the dawn of time. It is even more of a privilege to thank God that along different paths through the intervening decades the Lord has led us, on the vital concerns of this book, to the same place.

The point of Christian learning is to understand God's two books— Scripture and the world—and, with that understanding, to glorify God. The pages before you communicate that point very well. Pick them up, read them, test them by the Scriptures, reflect on their portrait of a loving God. In a word, think about it.

—Mark A. Noll
Francis A. McAnaney Professor of History,
University of Notre Dame

If you call out for insight
and raise your voice for understanding,
if you seek it like silver
and search for it as for hidden treasures,
then you will understand the fear of the LORD
and find the knowledge of God.

Proverbs 2:3–5

Introduction

This book is a plea to embrace serious thinking as a means of loving God and people. It is a plea to reject *either-or* thinking when it comes to head and heart, thinking and feeling, reason and faith, theology and doxology, mental labor and the ministry of love. It is a plea to see thinking as a necessary, God-ordained means of knowing God. Thinking is one of the important ways that we put the fuel of knowledge on the fires of worship and service to the world.

Knowing, Treasuring, Living—for the Glory of Christ

The ultimate goal of life is that God be displayed as glorious because of all that he is and all that he has made and done—especially the grace he has shown in the work of Christ. The way we glorify him is by knowing him truly, by treasuring him above all things, and by living in a way that shows he is our supreme treasure.

> It is my eager expectation and hope that . . . Christ will be honored in my body, whether by life or by death. For to me to live is Christ, and to die is gain. . . . To depart and be with Christ . . . is far better. . . . I count everything as loss because of the surpassing worth of knowing Christ Jesus my Lord. (Phil. 1:20–21, 23; 3:8)

Therefore, the main reason God has given us minds is that we might seek out and find all the reasons that exist for treasuring him *in* all things and *above* all things. He created the world so that *through* it and *above* it we might treasure him. The more we see of his surpassing greatness and knowledge and wisdom and power and justice and wrath and mercy and patience and goodness and grace and love, the more we will treasure him. And the more we treasure him, the more he is consciously and joyfully glorified. The point of this book is that *thinking* is a God-given means to that end.

How Is This Book Different?

There are other books about thinking. Good ones. Here are a few examples of how this one is different. It is less historical than Mark Noll's *Scandal of the Evangelical Mind*,[1] less punchy than Os Guinness's *Fit Bodies Fat Minds*,[2] less philosophical than J. P. Moreland's *Love Your God with All Your Mind*,[3] less vocational than James Sire's *Habits of the Mind*,[4] and less cultural than Gene Veith's *Loving God with All Your Mind*.[5]

So this book is *less* in lots of ways. What there is *more* of is biblical exposition. That's not a criticism of the other books. They are better than this one in many ways. They are what they were meant to be, and they are good. But I am a preacher—a Bible expositor. Most of my time is spent trying to figure out what the Bible means and how it applies to life. That's what this book will taste like.

Who Is the Book For?

Is it for students? Yes, if you agree with me that everybody should be a student. Meaning number two in the dictionary: STUDENT— "any person who studies, investigates, or examines thoughtfully." It's pretty hard to get through life without examining *something* thoughtfully. But mainly it's for the Christian—in or out of school— who wants to know God better, love him more, and care about people.

---

[1]Mark Noll, *The Scandal of the Evangelical Mind* (Grand Rapids: Eerdmans, 1994).

[2]Os Guinness, *Fit Bodies Fat Minds: Why Evangelicals Don't Think and What to Do About It* (Grand Rapids: Baker, 1994).

[3]J. P. Moreland, *Love Your God with All Your Mind: The Role of Reason in the Life of the Soul* (Colorado Springs: NavPress, 1997).

[4]James W. Sire, *Habits of the Mind: Intellectual Life as a Christian Calling* (Downers Grove, IL: InterVarsity, 2000).

[5]Gene Edward Veith Jr., *Loving God with All Your Mind: Thinking as a Christian in the Postmodern World*, rev. ed. (Wheaton, IL: Crossway, 2003). See also Richard Hughes, *How Christian Faith Can Sustain the Life of the Mind* (Grand Rapids: Eerdmans, 2001); Clifford Williams, *The Life of the Mind: A Christian Perspective* (Grand Rapids: Baker Academic, 2002).

Yes, I have concerns. For example, I hope this book will help rescue the victims of evangelical pragmatism, Pentecostal short-cuts, pietistic anti-intellectualism, pluralistic conviction aversion, academic gamesmanship, therapeutic Bible evasion, journalistic bite-sizing, musical mesmerizing, YouTube craving, and postmodern Jell-O juggling. In other words, I believe thinking is good for the church in every way.

Not to Overstate the Case

But I hate to sound snooty—which every book on thinking does. So see if this helps. It comes from a philosopher, Nicholas Wolterstorff, which makes its earthiness more compelling. He admits that *over*-intellectualism is a plague just like *anti*-intellectualism. *Over*-intellectualism sounds like this:

> If you use your hands or teach those who use their hands . . . you are inferior to those who use only their heads: practicing musicians are inferior to musicologists, painters are inferior to art historians, teachers of business are inferior to economists, teachers of preaching are inferior to theologians. The basic attitude was stated crisply by Aristotle . . . : "We think the master-workers in each craft are more honorable . . . than the manual workers."[6]

Not so, says Wolterstorff. He adds, "It's a strange attitude for Christians to hold, since Jesus was the son of a carpenter and since God is represented in the opening pages of Scripture as a maker, not a thinker."[7]

So I don't want to overstate the case. It's not about going to school or getting degrees or having prestige. It's not about the superiority of intellectuals. It's about using the means God has given us to know him, love him, and serve people. *Thinking* is one of those means. I would like to encourage you to think, but not to be too impressed with yourself when you do.

---

[6]Nicholas Wolterstorff, "Thinking with Your Hands," *Books and Culture* 15 (March/April 2009): 30.
[7]Ibid. Of course, when God speaks things into being, his word is virtually the same as his thought.

The Bible says, "If you . . . raise your voice for understanding, if you *seek it like silver* . . . then you will . . . find the knowledge of God" (Prov. 2:3–6). I need all the help I can get to love the knowledge of God more than the profits of silver. I assume you do too. So I wrote this book to remind myself of *the place of thinking in the pursuit of God*. Like a little echo of Calvin and Augustine, I say with them, "I count myself one of the number of those who write as they learn and learn as they write."[8] If you join me, I hope you find it helpful.

Mapping the Rest of the Book

If you're the type that gets help from a road map before you travel, read the rest of this introduction. If you prefer more surprises as you go along, skip it. Here's a sketch of where we are going.

I tell my own story in chapter 1. One of the reasons is that it seems honest to expose my background and influences and struggles. This gives you the chance to put my thoughts in a context and come to terms with some of my limitations. Another reason is that my own experience is, I think, typical of many evangelicals in the tensions I experienced in the awakening of the life of the mind. You may find yourself encouraged to follow a fellow struggler. Third, most of the issues the book raises emerge from my own interaction with God's world and God's Word. So my journey serves as a suitable portal onto the panorama we will study.

Chapter 2 tells the story of how Jonathan Edwards made a huge impact on my experience of the life of the mind. Though he has been dead over 250 years, his impact is still enormous on many thinkers today. My story of encountering him forms the basis for the rest of the book. What he provided for me was the deepest foundation for how thinking and feeling relate to each other. He did this through his vision of the Trinitarian nature of God.

---

[8]This is the way Calvin closed his "John Calvin to the Reader" at the beginning of his *Institutes*. The quote is also found in Augustine's *Letters* cxliii.2 (MPL 33. 585; tr. NPNF I. 490). John Calvin, *Institutes of the Christian Religion*, trans. Ford Lewis Battles, ed. John T. McNeill (Philadelphia: Westminster, 1960), 5.

In chapter 3 we turn from the more or less autobiographical focus in clarifying the aim of the book (chapters 1 and 2) to what I actually mean by the task of *thinking*. What I have in mind mainly is the amazing act of *reading*. The best reading of the most insightful literature (especially the Bible) involves serious thinking. That's the point of chapter 3.

Chapters 4 and 5 attempt to show *that* thinking functions (chapter 4) and *how* thinking functions (chapter 5) in the process of coming to faith in Jesus. One might infer from the pervasive effects of sin in laming our minds that thinking has no significant role in how God creates saving faith. But, in fact, we will see the crucial role of thinking both in coming to faith and in sustaining faith.

Having clarified the role of thinking in how we come to faith in Christ (chapters 4 and 5), we will turn in chapter 6 to the role of thinking in how we fulfill the Great Commandment—to love God. Jesus said that we should love God with all our *mind* (Matt. 22:37). Some have treated this as if it means "think hard and think accurately, and that act of thinking *is* loving God." But I doubt that.

I will suggest that loving God with the mind means that *our thinking is wholly engaged to do all it can to awaken and express the heartfelt fullness of treasuring God above all things.* Treasuring God is the essence of loving him, and the mind serves this love by comprehending (imperfectly and partially, but truly) the truth and beauty and worth of the Treasure. What is the biblical basis for this understanding of loving God with our minds? That's what chapter 6 is about.

But everything in chapters 1 through 6 would be pointless if real knowing is impossible, or if nothing is there to know. A common notion today is that knowledge of things outside our own mind is impossible. One of the names for this attitude is relativism. In chapters 7 and 8, I try to explain what this is and what Jesus thought about it. I argue in chapter 7 that relativism is neither intellectually compelling nor morally upright. Then in chapter 8, I try to build up your immune system against the intellectual virus of relativism by inoculating you, if you're willing, with seven harmful and immoral aspects of the disease. My aim is a deeply peaceful confidence and freedom to see and savor and speak the truth whose treasures are hidden in Jesus Christ.

But this hope-filled attitude toward the pursuit of Christ-exalting truth through the use of the mind has not been the mark of recent Christian history—at least not in America. A pervasive anti-intellectualism hangs in the air. In chapter 9, I try to give you a sense of this atmosphere. One way to look at chapters 9 through 11 is that they are my effort to show that the supposed biblical pillars for anti-intellectualism are very shaky. But the biblical foundations for a robust use of the mind for the sake of loving God and man are deep and strong.

Two passages of Scripture seem, on the face of it, to promote anti-intellectualism. One is Luke 10:21 where Jesus says, "You have hidden these things from the wise and understanding and revealed them to little children." We deal with this in chapter 10. The other is 1 Corinthians 1:20: "Has not God made foolish the wisdom of the world?" This is our focus in chapter 11. These two passages have become pillars in the house of anti-intellectualism. It is striking how similar these passages are in what they teach. But they prove to be shaky pillars indeed.

The upshot of our study of these "pillars" is that they are not warnings against careful, faithful, rigorous, coherent thinking in the pursuit of God. In fact, the way Jesus and Paul spoke these warnings compels us to engage in serious thinking even to understand them. And what we find is that pride is no respecter of persons—the serious thinkers may be humble. And the careless mystics may be arrogant.

The aim of this book is to encourage serious, faithful, humble thinking that leads to the true knowledge of God, which leads to loving him, which overflows in loving others. There is such a way of thinking that avoids the pitfalls of pride both among the common man and the most educated. In chapter 12 we catch a glimpse of it in Paul's amazing warning against the knowledge that puffs up. The focus here is on 1 Corinthians 8:1–3 and Romans 10:1–4. The lesson of chapter 12 is that thinking is dangerous and indispensable. Without a profound work of grace in the heart, thinking puffs up. But with that grace, thinking opens the door of humble knowledge. And that knowledge is the fuel of the fire of love for God and man. But if we turn away from serious thinking in our pursuit of God, that fire will eventually go out.

Finally, in chapter 13 we expand on the implication of chapter 12, that all thinking—all learning, all education, all schooling, formal or informal, simple or sophisticated—exists for the love of God and the love of man. We take the truth of 1 Corinthians 8:1–3 and apply it to the knowledge of God through his other "book," the created world of nature and human life.

The upshot is that the task of all Christian scholarship—not just biblical studies—is to study reality as a manifestation of God's glory, to speak and write about it with accuracy, and to savor the beauty of God in it, and to make it serve the good of man. It is an abdication of scholarship when Christians do academic work with little reference to God. If all the universe and everything in it exists by the design of an infinite, personal God, to make his manifold glory known and loved, then to treat any subject without reference to God's glory is not scholarship but insurrection.

In summary then, all branches of learning—and this book about thinking—exist ultimately for the purposes of knowing God, loving God, and loving man through Jesus Christ. And since loving man means ultimately helping him see and savor God in Christ forever, it is profoundly right to say all thinking, all learning, all education, and all research is for the sake of knowing God, loving God, and showing God. "For from him and through him and to him are all things. To him be glory forever. Amen" (Rom. 11:36).

Clarifying the Aim
of the Book

Indeed, thoughts and affections are
sibi mutuo causae—the mutual causes of each other:
"Whilst I mused, the fire burned" (Psalm 39:3);
so that thoughts are the bellows that kindle
and inflame affections; and then if they are inflamed,
they cause thoughts to boil;
therefore men newly converted to God,
having new and strong affections,
can with more pleasure think of God than any.

Thomas Goodwin

My Pilgrimage

All my life I have lived with the tension between thinking and feeling and doing.

The Move of '79

After twenty-two years of nonstop formal education and six years of college teaching, I left academia for the pastorate at age thirty-four. That was almost thirty years ago. I remember the night of October 14, 1979, when I wrote seven pages in my journal about the crisis in my soul concerning college teaching versus pastoral ministry. It was one of the most important days of my life—I can see that now.

It seemed to me then that these things—thinking and feeling and doing—would perhaps find a better balance in the church than in school. By "better" I mean a balance that would fit my gifts, and God's call, and people's needs, and the purposes of God for this world. I think I did the right thing. But I don't mean it would be right for everybody.

In fact, one of the purposes of this book is to celebrate the indispensable place of education in the cause of Christ. If every faculty member in the university or seminary did what I did, it would be tragic. I love what God did for me in academia for twenty-eight years, from ages six to thirty-four.

I am not among the number who looks back with dismay on what I was, or wasn't, taught. If I had it to do over again, I would take almost all the same classes with the same teachers and teach almost all the same classes. I didn't expect college and seminary and graduate school to teach me things that have to be learned on the job. If I have stumbled, it wasn't their fault.

The Painful Joy of Academia

Nor did I leave academia because it was spiritually stifling. On the contrary. All through college, and more so through seminary, and then even more in my six years of college teaching, my reading and thinking and writing made my heart burn with zeal for God. I have never been one of those who found the heart shrivel as God and his Word are known better. Putting more knowledge in my head about God and his ways was like throwing wood in the furnace of my worship. For me, seeing has meant savoring. And the clearer the seeing, the sweeter the savoring.

Not that there weren't tears. Some of my notions about God went up in the flames of biblical truth. It hurt. I would put my face in my hands some afternoons and weep with the pain of confusion. But, as the Native American proverb says, the soul would have no rainbow if the eye had no tears. Some joys are only possible on the other side of sorrow. It is true when the preacher says, "In much wisdom is much vexation, and he who increases knowledge increases sorrow" (Eccles. 1:18). But it is worth it.

And I don't mean that the seeing which led to savoring was easy. The work involved in figuring out what the Bible means when it talks about God is often agonizingly difficult. I know something of Luther's agonizing statement, "I beat importunately upon Paul at that place, most ardently desiring to know what St. Paul wanted."[1] I simply mean that when all is said and done, the work of thinking led me again and again to worship. Academia was life-giving for me.

[1]John Dillenberger, ed. *Martin Luther: Selections from His Writings* (Garden City, NY: Doubleday, 1961), 12.

Enflamed to Preach by Romans 9

I left in search of a new life of exultation over the truth. There is
an irony in the fact that what led to my leaving was a sabbatical in
which I wrote a book on Romans 9.[2] *The Justification of God* is the
most complicated, intellectually demanding book I have ever written. It deals with the most difficult theological issues and one of the
hardest texts in the Bible. Yet, ironically, the research and writing
of this book was what God used to enflame my heart for preaching
and pastoral ministry. Writing this most difficult book about God's
sovereignty was not dispiriting; it was incendiary. This was the God
I wanted more than anything to proclaim—not just explain.

Yet it was the explaining that set fire to the proclaiming. I have
not forgotten that. That is the main point of this book. I haven't forgotten because it is still true. "As I mused," says the psalmist, "the fire
burned; then I spoke with my tongue" (Ps. 39:3). Musing. Brooding.
Pondering. Thinking. That has been for me the pathway to seeing
and savoring and singing and speaking—and staying. Year after year,
this has been my work—prayer-saturated, Spirit-dependent *thinking*
about what God has revealed of himself to provide fuel for passion
and preaching.

Thinking is indispensable on the path to passion for God.
Thinking is not an end in itself. Nothing but God himself is finally
an end in itself. Thinking is not the goal of life. Thinking, like non-
thinking, can be the ground for boasting. Thinking, without prayer,
without the Holy Spirit, without obedience, without love, will puff
up and destroy (1 Cor. 8:1). But thinking under the mighty hand of
God, thinking soaked in prayer, thinking carried by the Holy Spirit,
thinking tethered to the Bible, thinking in pursuit of more reasons
to praise and proclaim the glories of God, thinking in the service
of love—such thinking is indispensable in a life of fullest praise to
God.

---

[2]John Piper, *The Justification of God: A Theological and Exegetical Study of Romans 9:1–23* (1983;
repr. Grand Rapids: Baker, 1993).

The Tension

And yet the tension remains. Thinking and feeling and doing jostle each other in my life, jockeying for more room. There never seems to be a satisfactory proportion. Should I be doing more, thinking more, feeling more, expressing more feeling? No doubt this discomfort is owing partly to quirks in my personality, factors in my background, and the remaining corruption in my heart.

But this tension is also due to a history of over-intellectualism and anti-intellectualism in the church; and it is due partly to a complexity in the Bible itself. Too often, the church has been ambivalent about "the life of the mind." America, in particular, has a long history of evangelical suspicion of education and intellectual labor. The most notable narration of this story for evangelicals is Mark Noll's *The Scandal of the Evangelical Mind*, whose first sentence is, "The scandal of the evangelical mind is that there is not much of an evangelical mind."[3]

The Lament of the Thinkers

Thirty years before Noll's indictment Harry Blamires wrote, "In contradistinction to the secular mind, no vital Christian mind plays fruitfully, as a coherent and recognizable influence, upon our social, political, or cultural life. . . . There is no Christian mind."[4] And since Noll, others have joined the lament. J. P. Moreland has a chapter called, "How We Lost the Christian Mind and Why We Must Recover It."[5] And Os Guinness has written *Fit Bodies Fat Minds: Why Evangelicals Don't Think and What to Do About It.*[6]

These friends are describing not just the world but the home I

---

[3]Mark Noll, *The Scandal of the Evangelical Mind* (Grand Rapids: Eerdmans, 1994), 3.

[4]Harry Blamires, *The Christian Mind: How Should a Christian Think?* (London: SPCK, 1963), 6.

[5]J. P. Moreland, *Love Your God with All Your Mind: The Role of Reason in the Life of the Soul* (Colorado Springs: NavPress, 1997), 19–40.

[6]Os Guinness, *Fit Bodies Fat Minds: Why Evangelicals Don't Think and What to Do About It* (Grand Rapids: Baker, 1994). "At root, evangelical anti-intellectualism is both a scandal and a sin. It is a scandal in the sense of being an offense and a stumbling block that needlessly hinders serious people from considering the Christian faith and coming to Christ. It is a sin because it is a refusal, contrary to the first of Jesus' two great commandments, to love the Lord our God with our minds" (10–11).

grew up in. As far as the world goes, R. C. Sproul has written that "we live in what may be the most anti-intellectual period in the history of Western civilization."[7] As far as my fundamentalist upbringing goes, Noll says that for the kind of thinking that embraces society, the arts, the human person, and nature—"for that kind of thinking the habits of mind fundamentalism encouraged can only be called a disaster."[8] It is not surprising perhaps then that I find myself pulled in different directions. For even Noll admits that there are amazing accomplishments for the good of the world brought about by the very impulses which, in part, undermined the deeper life of the mind.[9]

Knowledge: Dangerous and Liberating

But whatever I inherited in the atmosphere of my world and my home, the more mature tension I experience between thinking and feeling and doing is due largely to the Bible itself. There are some sentences in God's Word that make knowledge sound dangerous and others that make it sound glorious. For example, on the one hand, it says, "Knowledge puffs up, but love builds up" (1 Cor. 8:1 NET); and, on the other hand, it says, "You will know the truth, and the truth will set you free" (John 8:32). Knowing is dangerous. Knowing is liberating. And that is not an isolated paradox.

So what I want to do in this book is take you with me into the Bible itself to see how God has ordered this act of thinking in relation to other crucial acts in life. How does it relate to our believing, and worshiping, and living in this world? Why are there so many warnings about "knowledge" (1 Tim. 6:20), and "the wisdom of this world" (1 Cor. 3:19), and "philosophy" (Col. 2:8), and the "debased mind" (Rom. 1:28), and "the wise and understanding" who can't see (Luke 10:21), and those whose understanding is darkened (Eph. 4:18)?

---

[7] R. C. Sproul, "Burning Hearts Are Not Nourished by Empty Heads," *Christianity Today* 26, no 14 (September 3, 1982), 100.

[8] Noll, *Scandal of the Evangelical Mind*, 132.

[9] Ibid., 3. "An extraordinary range of virtues is found among the sprawling throngs of evangelical Protestants in North America, including great sacrifice in spreading the message of salvation in Jesus Christ, open-hearted generosity to the needy, heroic personal exertion on behalf of troubled individuals, and the unheralded sustenance of countless church and parachurch communities."

"Think Over What I Say"

In spite of all these warnings, the overwhelming message of the Bible is that knowing the truth is crucial. And *thinking*—eagerly and humbly using the mind God gave us, and using it well—is essential to knowing the truth.

Two passages of Scripture provide the main point of this book. The first is 2 Timothy 2:7, where Paul says to Timothy, "Think over what I say, for the Lord will give you understanding in everything." The command is that he think, consider, use his mind to try to understand what Paul means. And the reason Paul gives for this thinking is this: "For the Lord will give you understanding." Paul does not put these in tension: thinking on the one side and receiving the gift of understanding from God on the other side. They go together. Thinking is essential on the path to understanding. But understanding is a gift of God. That's the point of this book.

"Seek It like Silver"

The other passage is Proverbs 2:1–6. I'll boil it down to make it easier to see how similar it is to 2 Timothy 2:7. "If you . . . raise your voice for understanding, if you seek it like silver . . . then you will . . . find the knowledge of God. For the Lord gives wisdom; from his mouth come knowledge and understanding." The point is that we should seek understanding as a miser seeks silver. We should use our minds with eagerness and skill. What is the reason given? The same one Paul gave: "For the Lord gives wisdom." They go together—our seeking understanding and God's giving it. Seeking it like silver is essential to finding. But finding is a gift of God. That is the point of this book.

A story about Benjamin Warfield may make the point clear. Warfield taught at Princeton Seminary for thirty-four years until his death in 1921. He reacted with dismay toward those who saw opposition between prayer for divine illumination and rigorous thinking about God's written Word. In 1911 he gave an address to students with this exhortation: "Sometimes we hear it said that ten minutes on your knees will give you a truer, deeper, more operative knowledge of God than ten hours over your books. 'What!' is the appropriate response, 'than ten hours over your books, on your knees?'"[10] *Both-and.* Not *either-or.* That's the vision I am trying to encourage in this book.

Now, to Introduce a Friend and Lay a Foundation

In one sense the next chapter is an extension of this one because it tells the story of how one man made a huge impact on my experience of this *both-and* life. You could say it is a tribute to a friend I never knew personally. In fact, he's been dead over 250 years. He became for me an inspiration to be this kind of *both-and* person.

But in another sense, the next chapter is the basis for the rest of the book. What this friend provided for me was the deepest foundation for how thinking and feeling relate to each other. He did this through his vision of the Trinitarian nature of God. I hope you benefit from his vision as much as I have.

[10]Benjamin Warfield, "The Religious Life of Theological Students," in *The Princeton Theology*, ed. Mark Noll (Grand Rapids: Baker, 1983), 263.

Edwards's piety continued on in the revivalist tradition,
his theology continued on in academic Calvinism,
but there were no successors to his God-centered
worldview or his profoundly theological philosophy.
The disappearance of Edwards's perspective
in American Christian history has been a tragedy.

Mark Noll

2

Deep Help from a Dead Friend

Few people have helped me with the interconnection of thinking and feeling more than the eighteenth-century New England pastor and theologian Jonathan Edwards. I told my story of his influence in my life in the book *God's Passion for His Glory: Living the Vision of Jonathan Edwards*.[1] Here I will pay another debt.

Edwards without a Successor

Edwards, as almost every historian says, was among the greatest thinkers that America has ever produced, if not the greatest.[2] He embodied the *both-and* that this book is about. In fact, historian Mark Noll argues that no one since Edwards has embodied the union of mind and heart the way Edwards did.

> Edwards's piety continued on in the revivalist tradition, his theology continued on in academic Calvinism, but there were no successors to his God-centered worldview or his profoundly theological philosophy. The disappearance of Edwards's perspective in American Christian history has been a tragedy.[3]

---

[1]John Piper, *God's Passion for His Glory: Living the Vision of Jonathan Edwards* (Wheaton, IL: Crossway, 1998).

[2]Mark Noll, *The Scandal of the Evangelical Mind* (Grand Rapids: Eerdmans, 1994), 24. ". . . the greatest evangelical mind in American history and one of the truly seminal thinkers in Christian history."

[3]Mark Noll, "Jonathan Edwards's Moral Philosophy, and the Secularization of American Christian Thought," *Reformed Journal* 33, no. 2 (February 1983): 26.

In other words, theology and piety found a union in Edwards that has disappeared or is very rare. I hope this book will encourage some to pursue that union.

Trinitarian Thinking and Feeling

One of the gifts Edwards gave to me, which I had not found any-where else, was a foundation for human thinking and feeling in the Trinitarian nature of God. I don't mean that others haven't seen human nature rooted in God's nature. I simply mean that the way Edwards saw it was extraordinary. He showed me that human think-ing and feeling do not exist arbitrarily; they exist because we are in the image of God, and God's "thinking" and "feeling" are more deeply part of his Trinitarian being than I had realized.

Prepare to be boggled. Here is Edwards's remarkable description of how the persons of the Trinity relate to each other. Notice that God the Son stands forth eternally as a work of God's thought. And God the Spirit proceeds from the Father and the Son as the act of their joy.

> This I suppose to be the blessed Trinity that we read of in the Holy Scriptures. The *Father* is the deity subsisting in the prime, unorigi-nated and most absolute manner, or the deity in its direct existence. The *Son* is the deity generated by God's understanding, or having an idea of Himself and subsisting in that idea. The *Holy Ghost* is the deity subsisting in act, or the divine essence flowing out and breathed forth in God's infinite love to and delight in Himself. And I believe the whole Divine essence does truly and distinctly subsist both in the Divine idea and Divine love, and that each of them are properly distinct persons.[4]

In other words, God the Father has had an eternal image and idea of himself that is so full it *is* another Person standing forth—distinct as the Father's idea, yet one in divine essence. And God the Father and the Son have had an eternal joy in each other's excellence that car-ries so fully what they are that another Person stands forth, the Holy

---

[4]Jonathan Edwards, "An Essay on the Trinity," in *Treatise on Grace and Other Posthumously Published Writings*, ed. Paul Helm (Cambridge, UK: Clarke, 1971), 118.

Spirit—distinct as the Father and Son's delight in each other, yet one in divine essence. There never was a time when God did not experience himself this way. The three Persons of the Trinity are coeternal. They are equally divine.

Glorified by Being Known and Enjoyed

But the amazing reality for our purposes here is that God's existence as a Trinity of Persons is the foundation of human nature as head and heart, thinking and feeling, knowing and loving. We can see this even more remarkably when we watch Edwards draw out the connection between God's nature and how he designed us to glorify him. Notice how Edwards moves from God's intra-Trinitarian glory to the glory God aims to get in creation.

> God is glorified within himself these two ways: (1) by appearing . . . to himself in his own perfect idea [of himself], or in his Son, who is the brightness of his glory; (2) by enjoying and delighting in himself, by flowing forth in infinite . . . delight towards himself, or in his Holy Spirit.
>
> . . . So God glorifies himself towards the creatures also [in] two ways: (1) by appearing to . . . their understanding; (2) in communicating himself to their hearts, and in their rejoicing and delighting in, and enjoying the manifestations which he makes of himself. . . . God is glorified not only by his glory's being seen, but by its being rejoiced in. . . . [W]hen those that see it delight in it: God is more glorified than if they only see it; his glory is then received by the whole soul, both by the understanding and by the heart.
>
> God made the world that he might communicate, and the creature receive, his glory; and that it might [be] received both by the mind and heart. He that testifies his idea of God's glory [doesn't] glorify God so much as he that testifies also his approbation of it and his delight in it.[5]

The implications of this truth for this book are huge. It implies, for example, that if we are to live according to our nature as human

[5]Jonathan Edwards, "Miscellanies" in *The Works of Jonathan Edwards*, vol. 13, ed. Thomas Schafer (New Haven, CT: Yale University Press, 1994), 495 (Miscellany 448).

beings in the image of God, and if we are to glorify God fully, we must engage our mind in knowing him truly and our hearts in loving him duly. The *both-and* plea of this book is not a mere personal preference of mine. It is rooted in the nature of God's Trinitarian existence and in how he has created us to glorify him with mind and heart.

Clear Truth for the Sake of Strong Affections

Edwards set the pattern for us in seeking to awaken the affections, not with entertainment or hype but with clear views of truth. In other words, he made the work of thinking serve the experience of worship and love.

> I should think myself in the way of my duty to raise the affections of my hearers as high as possibly I can, provided that they are affected with nothing but truth, and with affections that are not disagreeable to the nature of what they are affected with.[6]

What an amazing example he was of the *both-and—strong emotions* for the glory of God based on *clear biblical views of the truth* of God. So you know it is not for any kind of academic gamesmanship when he said, "Get that knowledge of divine things that is within your power, even a doctrinal knowledge of the principles of the Christian religion."[7] This was not for show. This was the work of the mind for the sake of marveling at God and ministering in love.

I hope it is clear now that the emphasis of this book on thinking is not at the expense of feeling or delighting or loving. Both are essential to being human, and both are essential to glorifying God. And, while it is true that mind and heart are mutually enlivening,[8] it is also clear that the mind is mainly the servant of the heart. That is, the mind serves to know the truth that fuels the fires of the heart.

---

[6]Jonathan Edwards, "Some Thoughts Concerning the Revival," in *The Works of Jonathan Edwards*, vol. 4, *The Great Awakening*, ed. C. C. Goen (New Haven, CT: Yale University Press, 1972), 387.

[7]Jonathan Edwards, "A Spiritual Understanding of Divine Things Denied to the Unregenerate," in *The Works of Jonathan Edwards, Sermons and Discourse 1723–1729*, ed. Kenneth P. Minkema (New Haven: Yale University Press, 1997), 92.

[8]See Thomas Goodwin's explanation of this mutuality in chap. 6.

The apex of glorifying God is enjoying him with the heart. But this is an empty emotionalism where that joy is not awakened and sustained by true views of God for who he really is. That is mainly what the mind is for.

Turning from Autobiography to Explanation

In the next chapter we turn from the more or less autobiographical focus in clarifying the aim of the book (chapters 1 and 2) to what I actually mean by the task of *thinking*. Perhaps surprisingly for some, what I have in mind mainly, though not exclusively, is the amazing privilege of *reading*. The best reading of the most insightful literature (especially the Bible) involves serious thinking. That's what I want to demonstrate next.

Clarifying the Meaning of Thinking

When any new fact enters the human mind it must
proceed to make itself at home;
it must proceed to introduce itself to the
previous denizens of the house.
That process of introduction of new facts
is called thinking. And, contrary to what seems
to be quite generally supposed,
thinking cannot be avoided by the Christian man.[1]

J. Gresham Machen

[1]J. Gresham Machen, *What Is Faith?* (1937; repr. Edinburgh: Banner of Truth, 1991), 242.

3

Reading as Thinking

Thinking is such a broad concept that it can mean anything we do with our mind. So let me bring some focus to the way I am using the word. Mainly I am referring to the activity of the mind in reading and understanding what others have written, especially the Bible. Of course, there are thousands of other things that we think about. Indeed we should and must think about many other things. In chapters 12 and 13, I move farther out from my main focus to the life of the mind in the many branches of learning. But my main concern is how thinking relates to our pursuit of knowing and loving God.

God Has Revealed Himself through a Book

While all of God's creation serves to reveal him in some way, he has willed that the clearest and most authoritative knowledge of him this side of heaven come through his written Word, the Bible. That is why our focus will be there. The Bible is the main place that we come to know God, and the Bible is a book, and a book requires thinking. From the foundation of knowing God through this book, it is then possible to move out and think fruitfully about all of life.

What then does thinking involve when it comes to understanding texts in the Bible?

Thinking about What to Read

First, you make a mental choice to focus your mind on some passage. That choice involves thinking. Whether you consider several possibilities of what to read and weigh the pros and cons, or whether you are carried along by a more immediate impulse—in either case your mind is involved and you choose to focus on a text. Let's say you choose to focus on Matthew 7:7–12:

> Ask, and it will be given to you; seek, and you will find; knock, and it will be opened to you. For everyone who asks receives, and the one who seeks finds, and to the one who knocks it will be opened. Or which one of you, if his son asks him for bread, will give him a stone? Or if he asks for a fish, will give him a serpent? If you then, who are evil, know how to give good gifts to your children, how much more will your Father who is in heaven give good things to those who ask him! So whatever you wish that others would do to you, do also to them, for this is the Law and the Prophets.

After you find it in the Bible (which requires the use of your mind), then you read it.

What an amazing act of thinking reading is! My most moving introduction to the exciting world of serious reading came from Mortimer Adler's classic, *How to Read a Book*, which is still in print (and doing nicely at Amazon) seventy years after first being published in 1939.

It is hard to overstate the breadth of the world that will open up to you if you are gripped by Adler's vision of reading. Let me try to entice you to get his book and read it by giving a few of the sentences that I marked over forty years ago.

> The best teachers are the ones who make the fewest pretensions. . . . Perhaps, if we teachers were more honest about our own reading disabilities, less loath to reveal how hard it is for us to read and how often we fumble, we might get the students interested in the game of learning instead of the game of passing.[2]

---

[2]Mortimer Adler, *How to Read a Book* (1939; repr. New York: Simon & Schuster, 1967), 13. The numbers after the remaining quotes are the page references from this edition.

When teachers no longer know how to perform the function of reading books *with* their students, they are forced to lecture *at* them instead. (p. 57)

Reading is better or worse according as it is more or less active. (p. 22)

What for one man requires little or no effort may demand genuine exertion for another. (p. 29)

Most of us do not know what the limits of our comprehension are. We have never tried our powers to the full. It is my honest belief that *almost all the great books in every field are within the grasp of all normally intelligent men.* (p. 30)

Hobbes said: "If I read as many books as most men"—he meant "misread"—"I should be as dull-witted as they." (p. 40)

It is certainly better to gather a few crumbs which have dropped from the table than to starve in futile adoration of the feast we cannot reach. (p. 61)

Do not say you agree, disagree, or suspend judgment, until you can say, "I understand." (p. 267)

There is no point in winning an argument if you know or suspect you are wrong. (p. 245)

Adler is inspiring and wise in the vision he lays out for how to read. I encourage you, at whatever age, if you have not read the book, to get it and read it. His main point is that reading is active. It is thinking. And it is a mountain of treasures waiting to be mined. A good bit of what I have to say is influenced by him.

Reading as Thinking

When you read, your mind sees shapes on the page. We call them letters. By years of teaching and association you have learned (with your mind) that these shapes stand for sounds (vowels and conso-nants). You have also learned that, when grouped in certain ways (tens of thousands of ways), these letters make words that signify objects and persons and actions and descriptions and ideas and feelings.

You have learned (by the use of your mind) that thousands

of these words correspond to realities (milk, darkness, joy, love, mother). And you have learned that, since other people know what these words correspond to, you can communicate. Ideas that are inside another person's mind can be transferred through words into your mind.

This is one of the main goals of reading. I text you a message: "Meet you at the Hut at five." The aim of reading this message is not a mystical experience or a creative reconstruction. The aim is for my idea—my intention—to move from my mind to your mind. This takes thinking. We have done it so often that there is virtually no effort in this act of thinking. You construe the meaning of

- "meet" (go to the same place and find each other);
- "you" (that's *you*, not him or her or them, but you);
- "at" (that's in the very place designated, not a block away);
- "the" (there is more than one, but you and I share enough experience to know which is "the" one);
- "Hut" (that's our lingo for the pizza place in Dinky Town);
- "at" (the very time designated, not an hour earlier or later);
- "five" (not paces, not years hence, not the address, but "o'clock," and P.M.; we know this from our shared usage).

Your brain is really working as you read and construe the meaning of this message. But you are so good at it that there's no effort. Your mind is superbly trained for this. You could not have done this when you were two. The training of your mind has come a long way. And oh how much further it can go!

Working Hard to Understand

So reading involves thinking—the astonishing act of recognizing symbols and making connections that enable you to construe meaning. We recognize what a challenge this is only when we start to read more complex texts—texts that have unfamiliar words, or involved sentence structure, or logical connections that are not immediately clear. When that's the case, either we give up quickly or we think harder.

That is mainly what I have in mind by thinking—working hard with our minds to figure out meaning from texts. Then, of course, we go on from there to think how that meaning relates to other meanings from other texts and from experiences in life. On and on the mind goes, until we build a coherent view of the world so that we can live a life that is rooted in a true understanding of God's Word and its application to the world.

Do unto Authors as You Would Have Them Do unto You

At the root of this coherent worldview and the process of being rooted in the Bible is the hard work of understanding what an author intends to communicate. We can call this "thinking an author's thoughts after him." This is the golden rule of reading: "Do unto *authors* as you would have them do unto you." Authors want to be understood, not misunderstood. So, for the reader, the golden rule of reading implies: work hard with your mind to understand what an author intended to convey.

When I write something, I generally have an idea that I would like others to grasp. If they construe my sentences in a way that is different from what I intend, then either I have written poorly or they have read poorly. Or both. But in either case, I am frustrated, because the aim of writing (except for liars and spies) is to be understood. So the aim of reading should ordinarily be to understand what the writer wants understood. To ignore that aim is to break the golden rule of reading.

I want my notes and contracts and love letters to be understood as I intend them. So that's also the way I should *read*. If I write, "I'm allergic to apple peels," don't tell the cook: "John doesn't eat apples." That's not what I said and not what I meant. Tell the cook to peel the apples. And when I get your note, "I'm allergic to orange peels," I will tell the cook not to grind the peels into the smoothie. That's the golden rule of reading—to work hard at understanding from words and sentences what an author meant to convey.

The Precious Gift of Grammar

Now back to the focus of our attention in Matthew 7:7–12. We are struck immediately with the fact that thinking must deal not only with words but with words in a particular order. For example, our mind must do something with the fact that "Ask" is the first word: "*Ask*, and it will be given to you." Whether we know the terminology or not, we have learned that this is a *verb* and that when verbs come first in English we usually are dealing with an *imperative*—a command or an exhortation. If you say, "I ask . . . " (and the word "ask" is in the second position, not the first), you are telling me what you are doing. If you say, "Ask . . . " (with the word "ask" in the first position), you typically are telling me to do something.

Whether or not we have ever studied this rule or have ever heard of the terms *verb*, *grammar*, or *imperative*, our mind has absorbed such rules and usages, and we know how to understand them. If we don't, we will have to think harder. What a precious gift it is to a child when he is taught these things by practice and precept from the time he is a baby.

Obvious Connections

Now it starts to really get interesting. That's the way thinking is. Rules about word order and the use of specific terms do not always tell us by themselves how to understand a sentence. Typically it's the words and the connections and the content together that make the point. For example, the word *and* does not usually mean: "and the result will be that." But that's what Jesus wants us to understand when he says, "Ask, *and* it will be given to you." He means, "Ask, *and the result will be that* it will be given to you." Our minds pick this up because of the content of what Jesus says as well as the word order and the way "and" can be used. The imperative "ask" followed by "it will be given" tells our brain (in this language system) that the gift is the result of the asking.

Again, you probably are so well taught that seeing this required almost no effort at all. You didn't pause when you were reading and say, "I just observed that 'ask' is the first word, and so this likely is an imperative, and it is followed by a promise that God will give what I ask, and so the promise is the result of the asking." Your mind did all that unconsciously. That's good. That level of thinking is usually easy. You have been well trained.

The Benefits of Deferred Gratification

In fact, we should pause here and remind ourselves that all training is painful and frustrating on the way to skills that later become second nature and lead to greater joy. The person who will not embrace the pain and frustration will remain at lower levels of achievement and joy. For example, learning to drive a car is tense. You have to remember so many things at the same time, especially if the car has a manual transmission—look both ways, take foot off accelerator, apply brake, push in clutch, change gears, let out clutch, put on blinker, turn wheel, push accelerator, and so on. It all feels uncertain and scary. But if you give up, you will forfeit the joys of driving where you please and being able to carry on a conversation while doing so, which happens only when driving has become second nature.

So it is with piano playing, and fly casting, and throwing a ball, and knitting, and learning a foreign language, and reading great books. At one point these tasks were all difficult and awkward. Learning the skill and practicing it was not fun. The joy is on the other side of the hard work. This is basic to all growing up. Part of maturity is the principle of deferred gratification. If you cannot embrace the pain of learning but must have instant gratification, you forfeit the greatest rewards of life.

So it is with reading the Bible. The greater riches are for those who will work hard to understand all that is really there. There are hundreds of connections and meanings and implications in the Bible that do not leap off the page at first reading—at least not for me. I have to slow down and start asking questions about the words and the connections. That is, thinking has to become intentional.

Up till now most of our thinking about Matthew 7:7–12 has been spontaneous and intuitive. We worked so long for the first ten years of our lives at learning how to speak and listen and read that we can now do it effortlessly. That is one of the great joys of education. And when I say *education* I mean learning, whether in school or out of school. Schooling is not the same as education.

But now we realize that our reading ability—our thinking ability—which serves us so well 90 percent of the time, does not see all that the Bible has to say. There comes a point when we choose to be intentional about our thinking, so that we grow in what we see and understand. If we don't choose to think harder, we will settle for an adolescent level of understanding the rest of our lives.

Asking Questions Is the Key to Understanding

One of the best honors I received during my six years of teaching college Bible classes was a t-shirt. My teaching assistant made it. On the back it said, "Asking questions is the key to understanding."

When I speak of becoming intentional about thinking harder, that's mainly what I mean: asking questions and working hard with our minds to answer them. Therefore, learning to think fruitfully about biblical texts means forming the habit of asking questions.[3] The kinds of questions you can ask of a text are almost endless:

- Why did the author use that word?
- Why did he put it here and not there?
- How does he use that word in other places?
- How is that word different from this other one he could have used?
- How does the combination of these words affect the meaning of that word?

---

[3]For more examples of what I mean by this habit, see "Brothers, Query the Text" in John Piper, *Brothers, We Are Not Professionals* (Nashville: Broadman, 2002), 73–80.

- Why does that statement follow this one?
- Why did he connect these statements with the word *because* or the word *therefore* or the word *although* or the words *in order that*? Is this logical?
  - How does it fit with what another author in the Bible says?
  - How does it fit with my experience?

Is the Habit of Asking Questions Respectful?

Some may wonder if asking questions of the text is a respectful way to read the Bible. It can be. Or it may not be. An illustration may clarify. Near the time of Jesus' birth, an angel came to Mary and to John the Baptist's father with predictions about what was going to happen. Both Mary and Zechariah asked a question about what the angel had said. But the angel was angry with Zechariah, not Mary. Why?

It had to do with the attitude of their hearts in asking their questions. The angel said to Zechariah, "Do not be afraid, Zechariah, for your prayer has been heard, and your wife Elizabeth will bear you a son, and you shall call his name John" (Luke 1:13). But Zechariah was old and his wife was barren. He was skeptical. In fact he was unbelieving. He expressed this with a question, "How shall I know this? For I am an old man, and my wife is advanced in years" (Luke 1:18).

The angel did not like this response. Zechariah did not ask humbly how God would do this. He was not submissive and trusting in his question. So the angel said, "I am Gabriel. I stand in the presence of God, and I was sent to speak to you and to bring you this good news. And behold, you will be silent and unable to speak until the day that these things take place, because you did not believe my words, which will be fulfilled in their time" (Luke 1:19–20).

But Mary's heart was different when she asked her question. The angel had said to her, "Do not be afraid, Mary, for you have found favor with God. And behold, you will conceive in your womb and bear a son, and you shall call his name Jesus" (Luke 1:30–31). Mary, of course, was perplexed and could not understand how this could be. So she asked, "How will this be, since I am a virgin?" (Luke 1:34). Instead of getting angry at her, the angel answered her question as far as he could: "The Holy Spirit will come upon you, and the power of the Most High will overshadow you; therefore the child to be born will be called holy—the Son of God" (Luke 1:35).

"Who Are You, O Man, to Answer Back to God?"

Not all question asking is good. It depends on the attitude. Is there a submission to the Word of God and a readiness to obey God when we understand what he wants of us? Is there a willingness to embrace the mysteries of God if something is plain but over our head?

One other example of the wrong kind of question is found in response to Paul's writing something very mysterious. He says, "[God] has mercy on whomever he wills, and he hardens whomever he wills" (Rom. 9:18). To this someone answers back, "Why does he still find fault? For who can resist his will?" Paul hears in this question a cynical questioning of God. So he answers, "But who are you, O man, to answer back to God?" (Rom. 9:19–20).[4]

There is a humble and submissive kind of question that is eager to understand and believe and obey the truth. And there is academic gamesmanship and unbelieving cynicism and indifferent dismissal. When I plead for the habit of asking questions, I mean humble questioning that expresses eagerness to grow and to uncover truth. I mean the habit that Jesus had already when he was twelve years old. "After three days they found him in the temple, sitting among the teachers, listening to them and *asking them questions*" (Luke 2:46).

The Fruitful Crutch

You may also wonder if this is a *fruitful* way to read—with habitual question asking. I can imagine someone saying: "Aren't these things obvious? Do we have to be so self-consciously *thought*ful when we

---

[4]The Greek word for "answer back" (ἀνταποκρινόμενος) seems to have the connotation of objecting against what was said, as the only other use in the New Testament (Luke 14:6) shows.

read the Bible?" No, you don't have to be. You may be very insightful without this practice. I mean that. There are people who can see in a flash what takes me hours of pondering (that is, thinking).

A professor asked me once about the processes I use to help me think, "Isn't all that a crutch?" I simply said, "Yes. Because when it comes to thinking fruitfully about God's fathomless Word I feel like a cripple. I need all the help I can get." I am usually dull and unperceptive when I read the Bible. So I pray earnestly that the Lord will incline my heart to his word (Ps. 119:36) and open my eyes to see wonders (Ps. 119:18). When I do that, the impulse God gives me (through his Word) is: "Think over what I say" (2 Tim. 2:7). Dig for understanding. "Seek it like silver" (Prov. 2:4). The Lord never says, "Stop thinking about my Word; I'll tell you what this means."

Going Deeper with Different Questions

Let me give you a little quiz to see if all that's precious and powerful in Matthew 7:7–12 is intuitively obvious to you. Did you notice that, after saying God would answer when we ask, seek, and knock, Jesus compared God to a human father who would not give his son a stone or a serpent when the son asks for bread and fish? I'm sure you did. Good.

Did you notice that God is said to be "much more" willing to give good things to his children when we ask him? Good. That's very good news. It will change our lives if we believe it.

But what if you ask the question, "Does Jesus promise that our heavenly Father always gives just what we ask for?" Hmmm. I'll have to reread to make sure. Well, it doesn't say that in so many words. Ask. Seek. Knock. Receive. Find. Door opened. But it doesn't say precisely *what* we receive and find. What about the human father? Does it say he gives exactly what his son asks? Check it. No. It says what he *won't* give—a stone and a snake.

Now this is worth thinking about. It seems that the point of this text is that God really loves to give when we ask. He is not stingy. He is not bothered when we come. He is eager to give. And he doesn't toy with us. He doesn't put rocks in our lunchbox, or snakes in our Happy Meal. He gives us what is good for us. That seems to be the point.

But what if we ask for something that is bad for us? My little son Benjamin once asked for a cracker, and when I opened the box they were moldy. I told him they had fuzz on them. He wasn't sure what I was talking about and said, "I'll eat the fuzz." But I didn't give them to him. He got some other treat that day. Maybe not what he preferred. But it was good for him. He asked. I gave. But not the exact request. I love him too much for that.

Of course this raises all kinds of questions about prayer and what other texts teach. That's the point. We are off and running with our questions. And the more questions we work hard to answer, the deeper we will know Jesus and our Father in heaven and how they work in the world.

"Therefore"—the Key to Many Treasures

So far so good. Maybe you saw all that in a flash and didn't have to ponder as long as I did or ask as many questions. But here is one last part of the quiz: Did you notice the word *so* at the beginning of verse 12? Did it send out a clear and compelling message about the relationship between Jesus' teaching on prayer, on the one hand, and the Golden Rule, on the other hand? It looks like this: "How much more will your Father who is in heaven give good things to those who ask him! So whatever you wish that others would do to you, do also to them."

The word *so* is not a throwaway word here. It is doing very serious work. Another way to translate it is "therefore." "God will answer your prayers and give you what's really good for you; *therefore* treat others the way you would like to be treated." I read this for years and never saw that connection. I saw it only because some teacher told me to start asking questions.

Why is that word *so* there? What does it tell me about the relationship between God's answering my prayers and my loving other people?

Seeing this connecting word *so* set me to thinking. And without thinking I would not have seen what I was about to see. Without thinking I would not grow in my understanding of what Jesus wants to tell me.

Perhaps you might want to pause before reading on and think through for yourself how this *so* is working here. How does what Jesus has just said lead to what he says after the *so*? How does the promise of Matthew 7:11 empower the command of verse 12?

Here's my attempt to think and pray my way into this text (which does not mean I am infallible). Treating others the way I would like to be treated is hard. It requires a good bit of self-denial. It means putting the good of others before my own immediate comfort and pleasure. Suppose the other person is being mugged. He is crying for help. So I ask, What if it were me? Would I want someone to try to help me? Yes. Is it dangerous to try to help? Yes. That's hard. Jesus knows it's hard. So he is helping us do the hard thing by telling us something with this word *so*.

He is saying: "You have a Father in heaven. He will give you what you need. He will help you. He really loves to answer when you call. He doesn't give you a stone or a snake. He is strong and he is wise and he is on your side when you love others. *Therefore*, trust him and take the risk. Do what you would like someone to do for you in this situation." In other words, the word, *therefore* (*so*), is meant by Jesus to empower the risks of love.[5]

Logic for the Sake of Love

This is incredibly important for real, practical Christian living. And it is profoundly dependent on thinking correctly. This book is not a book on logic, but I can't help but take a moment to point out that

---

[5]The practical implications of this kind of thinking are everywhere in the Bible. Just consider these uses of the word *therefore*. "*Therefore* do not be anxious about tomorrow" (Matt. 6:34). "Fear not, *therefore*" (Matt. 10:31). "*Therefore* . . . we have peace with God" (Rom. 5:1). "Let not sin *therefore* reign in your mortal body" (Rom. 6:12). "There is *therefore* now no condemnation for those who are in Christ Jesus" (Rom. 8:1). "*Therefore* let us not pass judgment on one another any longer" (Rom. 14:13). "*So then*, whether we live or whether we die, we are the Lord's" (Rom. 14:8). "*So* glorify God in your body" (1 Cor. 6:20). "Therefore, my beloved brothers, be steadfast, immovable, always abounding in the work of the Lord" (1 Cor. 15:58). "*Therefore* . . . we do not lose heart" (2 Cor. 4:1).

whenever you see the word *therefore* or the word *because* in the Bible, God is summoning logic to his service.

By *logic*—or you could use the word *reason*—I mean the way of thinking that enables you to see how the word *therefore* works and that keeps you from using it wrongly. For example, when logic or reason is working well, you don't say things like: "All dogs have four legs. This horse has four legs. *Therefore*, this horse is a dog." If you heard this you would say it's not true. And the reason it's not true is that the conclusion does not follow from the premises. "All dogs have four legs" doesn't mean *only* dogs have four legs. And therefore the premise doesn't lead you to believe that a horse is a dog. Other animals have four legs besides dogs.

One reason why this is important in reading the Bible is that the inspiration of the Bible implies that every time you read a *therefore* you may know for sure that the premises really do lead to the conclusion. That means you can go back and learn profound things about how such conclusions come about. The conclusion that we are to treat others the way we would like to be treated is built on premises. Massive, unshakable premises. Jesus means for us to see them.

Being logical at Matthew 7:12 is entirely in the service of being loving. This logic is not cold. It is a furnace driving the engine of love. Jesus does not say "therefore" for nothing. He means for us to see it, and think about it, and go back to the premises of God's fatherly care, and believe it, and be strengthened by it in the risky business of loving others.

Jesus expects that the logic of this passage, together with the use of our minds, along with the power of the Holy Spirit, will actually change our lives and make us radically loving people. That is what thinking is for.

If You Are Not an Intuitive Genius

It is possible that you may see such things without thinking—that is, you may see them immediately and intuitively without any self-conscious work of asking questions and thinking about answers. If so, you are one in a thousand and should be on your knees every day thanking God for such a gift. Then you should tremble at such a joyful burden because "everyone to whom much was given, of him much will be required" (Luke 12:48).

For the other 999 of us, the implications are becoming clearer: we need to think in order to receive what God has to give us from the Bible. For most people, what Paul said to Timothy still holds true: "*Think over* what I say, for the Lord will give you understanding in everything" (2 Tim. 2:7). For most of us, the counsel of Proverbs is still essential: "Seek [understanding] like silver and search for it as for hidden treasures. . . . For the LORD gives wisdom" (Prov. 2:4–6). These texts really mean that God gives the treasures of his wisdom through the tenacious task of our thinking.

Thinking Is More, but Not Less

What I have done in this chapter is illustrate what I mean by thinking. There is more to it, but I hope you get the idea. We observe carefully. We ask questions. And we work hard with our minds to try to answer the questions. And we weave the answers into an ever more extensive fabric of understanding that helps us live lives of love to the glory of Jesus Christ.[6]

The Role of Thinking in Becoming a Christian

The next two chapters attempt to show *that* thinking functions (chapter 4) and *how* thinking functions (chapter 5) in the process of coming to faith in Jesus. Both these chapters are set against the bleak backdrop of the deadening, darkening, destructive effects of

---

[6]I haven't devoted a section to the formal rules of logic because it seems to me that realistically most people do not learn to be logical and rational by reading books on logic but by asking questions and thinking hard as they interact with reasonable people (especially parents, while growing up) and as they read books that embody the truest way of thinking. I believe if you will look long and hard at the way each passage in the Bible is written, and if you ask relentlessly why the words and sentences are connected the way they are, you absorb the logic of heaven and grow in the truth that leads to love.

sin on our minds. It would be easy to infer from the pervasive effects of sin in laming our minds that thinking has no significant role in how God creates saving faith. But what we will see is that thinking is essential not just after faith, when we have embraced the Bible as God's Word, but also before faith in the very process of becoming a Christian.

Coming to Faith through Thinking

The Pharisees and Sadducees came, and to test [Jesus]
they asked him to show them a sign from heaven.
He answered them, "When it is evening, you say,
'It will be fair weather, for the sky is red.' And in the morning,
'It will be stormy today, for the sky is red and threatening.'
You know how to interpret the appearance of the sky,
but you cannot interpret the signs of the times.
An evil and adulterous generation seeks for a sign,
but no sign will be given to it except the sign of Jonah."

Matthew 16:1–4

4

Mental Adultery
Is No Escape

Since this book is mainly about how Christians use their minds in the pursuit of God, it is important to talk about how the mind is involved in becoming a Christian in the first place. How does the act of thinking relate to the rise of faith? Do you have to suspend your reason in order to put faith in Christ? If thinking about Jesus is the pathway to faith, how does the work of the Holy Spirit fit in?

Hebraic versus Hellenistic Thinking?

When I was in seminary, there was much talk about Hellenistic (or Greek) thinking versus Hebraic thinking. An example of Hellenistic thinking is Aristotelian logic, which has the syllogism at its foundation: "All men are mortal; Plato is a man; therefore, Plato is mortal."[1] The point of this distinction between Hebraic and Hellenistic thinking was to argue that the Bible tends to be Hebraic, but modern Western people tend to be the heirs of Hellenistic thinking. So if we use Aristotelian logic in understanding the Scriptures, it must be

[1]In his *Prior Analytics*, Aristotle defines syllogism as "a discourse in which, certain things having been supposed, something different from the things supposed results of necessity because these things are so" (24b, 18–20). Available at http://classics.mit.edu/Aristotle/prior.1.i.html (accessed February 9, 2010).

because we are historically uninformed insensitive to the original context and The Bible does not have its roots in linear, Aristotelian (sometimes called "Western") logic, they said, but in relational, experiential knowledge.

I always thought those generalizations and distinctions were misleading and unhelpful. Mainly they didn't smell right. It is a great philosophical gift to grow up in a Bible-saturated home where the atmosphere of Scripture gets into your bones. In a hundred places one can sniff something foul before the irrational flaw is obvious. One is spared many wasted years of dead-end detours.

The problem is that the Bible itself made these distinctions between Hellenistic and Hebraic unworkable—at least in the way they were being bandied about in those days. Take Matthew 16:1–4, for example. This text is one of the reasons I wasn't impressed with those distinctions.

> The Pharisees and Sadducees came, and to test [Jesus] they asked him to show them a sign from heaven. He answered them, "When it is evening, you say, 'It will be fair weather, for the sky is red.' And in the morning, 'It will be stormy today, for the sky is red and threatening.' You know how to interpret the appearance of the sky, but you cannot interpret the signs of the times. An evil and adulterous generation seeks for a sign, but no sign will be given to it except the sign of Jonah." So he left them and departed.

Aristotelian Pharisees

What is Jesus saying to these Pharisees and Sadducees? He says in verse 2, "When it is evening, you say, 'It will be fair weather, for the sky is red.'" What does that mean? It means that these Hebraic Pharisees and Sadducees are thinking in so-called Aristotelian syllogisms.

> Premise 1: Red skies in the evening portend fair weather.
> Premise 2: This evening the skies are red.
> Conclusion: Therefore, the weather will be fair.

Then in the first part of verse 3 they show that they are thinking this way again. They say in the morning, "It will be stormy today, for the sky is red and threatening." Again they are thinking in this so-called Western, linear way:

> Premise 1: Red skies in the morning portend stormy weather.
> Premise 2: This morning the skies are red.
> Conclusion: Therefore, the weather will be stormy.

Jesus responded to this use of observation and reasoning: "You know how to interpret the appearance of the sky." In other words, "You know how to use your eyes and your minds to draw right conclusions when it comes to the natural world." So he *approves* of their use of empirical observation and rational deliberation. In fact, it's precisely this approval that makes the following disapproval valid.

He says at the end of verse 3, "But you cannot interpret the signs of the times." And when he says, "You *cannot*," he does not mean they don't have the sensory and rational capacities to do what needs to be done. He just showed them that they *do* in fact have the sensory and rational capacities to do what needs to be done. The Pharisees and Sadducees are very adept at observation and deliberation when it comes to getting along in this world.

Adulterous Irrationality

Why then *can't* they use those same faculties to interpret the signs of the times? Answering this question will open a window on how faith and reason are connected. Here are people who seem to have competent reasoning abilities but are not able to use them to come to faith in Jesus. What's wrong? Why is their thinking working so well at the natural level but so badly when it comes to perceiving the presence of God in Christ?

The answer is given in verse 4: "An evil and *adulterous* generation seeks for a sign, but no sign will be given to it except the sign of

Jonah." What does this mean? What does being *adulterous* have to do with their inability to use their eyes and their minds to interpret the signs—that is, to recognize Jesus for who he is?

Here's the point of calling them "adulterous." Jesus described himself elsewhere as the bridegroom (Matt. 9:15; 25:1ff.) who has come into the world to obtain his bride—his chosen people. He is thinking corporately, not individually. The church as a whole is the bride of Christ. He is the covenant "husband" of the whole.

But the people who thought they were the people of God were, by and large, unwilling to have him as their husband. He was not what they expected, and they did not want to be his people or his bride (see Luke 14:18–20). They were, in that sense, *adulterous*. Their hearts went after other spouses—other gods, other treasures (see Luke 16:14; Matt. 6:5). Jesus points out that the leaders of the Jewish people who were supposed to be his bride had an ongoing love affair with the praise of men (Matt. 6:5) and money (Luke 16:14) and self (Luke 18:9). They were spiritual adulterers.

This is why the Pharisees are asking for a sign. They want to give the impression that there is not enough evidence that Jesus is the Messiah and so they are justified in not receiving him as their bridegroom. But, in fact, the problem is that they don't *want* him as their bridegroom. They are dominated by a spirit of adultery. They prefer other sources of satisfaction.

The Roots of Irrationality

Jesus' response is to show them that they have all the signs they need, and that they are perfectly able to use their senses and their minds to make valid judgments when they are trying to draw inferences about *what they want*. They really want to see true signs about the safety of the seas because they love their lives. So their minds are in full gear to think clearly about sunrise and sunset.

But not so when it comes to thinking clearly about Jesus. The explanation of their skepticism about Jesus is not lack of evidence or lack of rational powers. The explanation is: they are adulterous. Jesus says their hearts are *evil* (v. 4). And their evil hearts disorder their rational powers and make them morally incapable of reasoning rightly about Jesus.

Jesus was not the only one who saw the way sin disorders our thinking. This is what Paul said in Ephesians 4:18 about fallen man in general: "They are darkened in their understanding, alienated from the life of God because of the ignorance that is in them, *due to their hardness of heart.*" In other words, at the bottom of human irrationality ("darkened in their understanding") and at the bottom of spiritual ignorance ("the ignorance that is in them") is *hardness of heart.* That is, our self-centered hearts distort our reason to the point where we cannot use it to draw true inferences from what is really there. If our disapproval of God's existence is strong enough, our sensory faculties and our rational faculties will not be able to infer that he is there.

In 2 Corinthians 3:14 Paul says the mind is "hardened" (*epōrōthē*). In 1 Timothy 6:5 he calls the mind "depraved" (*diephthar-menōn*). And in Romans 1:21 he says that thinking has become "futile" (*emaraiōthēsan*) and "darkened" (*eskotisthē*) and "foolish" (*asunetos*) because men "by their unrighteousness suppress the truth" (Rom.1:18). In other words, unrighteousness disorders our capacity to think (see also 2 Tim. 3:8; 4:2–4). The corruption of our hearts is the deepest root of our irrationality.

We are an adulterous generation. We love man-centered error more than Christ-exalting truth, and our rational powers are taken captive to serve this adulterous love. This is what Jesus exposed when he said, "You know how to interpret the appearance of the sky, but you cannot interpret the signs of the times." In other words, "Your mind functions just fine when seeking out partners in adultery (like comfort and safety on the sea as more precious than Christ), but it cannot see the signs of Christ-exalting truth."

Nevertheless, "Think Over What I Say"

The fact that our minds cannot see the signs of Christ-exalting truth would seem to lead to the conclusion that reasoning and thinking are useless in coming to faith in Christ. But that is not the conclusion the Bible comes to.

The New Testament speaks throughout of the use of our minds in the process of Christian conversion and growth and obedience. For example, at least ten times in the book of Acts, Luke says that Paul's strategy was to "reason" with people in his effort to convert them to Christ and build them up (Acts 17:2, 4, 17; 18:4, 19; 19:8, 9; 20:7, 9; 24:25). And Paul said to the Corinthians that he would rather speak five understandable words with his mind to instruct others than ten thousand unintelligible words in a tongue (1 Cor. 14:19). He said to the Ephesians, "When you read this, you can perceive my insight into the mystery of Christ" (Eph. 3:4). In other words, engaging the mind in the mental task of reading is a pathway into the mysteries of God.

Here we meet again the main point of this book about the relationship between our thinking and God's illuminating. Recall that in 2 Timothy 2:7 Paul says, "*Think* over what I say, for *the Lord will give you understanding* in everything." So many people swerve off the road to one side of this verse or the other. Some stress "Think over what I say." They emphasize the indispensable role of reason and thinking. And they often minimize the supernatural role of God in making the mind able to see and embrace the truth. Others stress the second half of the verse: "for the Lord will give you understanding in everything." They emphasize the futility of reason without God's illumining work.

But Paul will not be divided that way. And I am writing this book to plead that we follow Paul in this—that we not swerve to the right or the left, but embrace both human thinking and divine illumination. For Paul it was not *either-or*, but *both-and*. "*Think* over what I say, for *the Lord will give you understanding* in everything." Notice the little word *for*. This is one of those crucial connecting words that makes us ask the question: Why is it here? It beckons us to ponder.

This word "for" means that the willingness of God to give us understanding is the *ground* of our thinking, not the substitute for it. Paul does not say, "God gives you understanding, so don't waste your time thinking over what I say." Nor does he say, "Think hard over what I say because it all depends on you, and God does not illumine the mind." No. He emphatically makes God's gift the ground of our effort. He makes God's giving light the reason for our pursuing light. "Think over what I say, *for* the Lord will give you understanding."

There is no reason to believe that a person who thinks without prayerful trust in God's gift of understanding will get it. And there is no reason to believe that a person who waits for God's gift of understanding without thinking about his Word will get it either. *Both-and*. Not *either-or*.

The Good Soil Understands

Paul commands us to think about what he says. Use your mind. Engage your reasoning powers when you hear the Word of God. In another place, Jesus warned what happens if we don't and what blessing may come if we do. He told a parable about four soils (Matt. 13:3–9). When the seed of the Word is sown on the first three, it bears no fruit. Only the fourth soil bears fruit. What's the difference?

We get a glimpse of the problem when we compare the first and fourth soils. Jesus said concerning the seed sown on the first soil, the path: "When anyone hears the word of the kingdom and *does not understand it*, the evil one comes and snatches away what has been sown in his heart" (Matt. 13:19). Jesus focuses on the failure to understand. Not understanding the Word results in the Word being snatched away. Therefore, understanding with the mind is not optional. It's crucial to conversion and fruit-bearing. Our lives hang on it. Then concerning the seed sown on the fourth soil, the good soil, he says, "This is the one who hears the word *and understands it*. He indeed bears fruit and yields, in one case a hundredfold, in another sixty, and in another thirty" (Matt. 13:23). The difference between the soil that is lifeless and the soil that bears fruit is understanding.

It is true, as Paul says in Romans 10:17, that "faith comes from hearing, and hearing through the word of Christ." So hearing is important. But Jesus says that hearing *without understanding* produces nothing. When we hear the Word of God, Paul says, we must "think over" what we hear. Otherwise, we will fall under the indictment of Jesus: "Hearing they do not hear, nor do they understand" (Matt. 13:13).

No Faith without Thinking

So, even though our natural minds are depraved and darkened and foolish, the New Testament demands that we use them in coming to faith and leading people to faith and in the process of Christian growth and obedience. There is no way to awaken faith or strengthen faith that evades thinking.

But how can that be, in view of how our sinfulness distorts our thinking? How does it work? How do thinking and divine illumination relate to each other in the awakening of faith? Before we try to answer that, we need to clarify what faith is. That's what we will do in the next chapter—describe saving faith and how it rises from the use of human thinking and divine illumination.

The god of this world has blinded the minds of
the unbelievers, to keep them from seeing the light
of the gospel of the glory of Christ, who is the image of God.
For what we proclaim is not ourselves, but Jesus Christ as Lord,
with ourselves as your servants for Jesus' sake.
For God, who said, "Let light shine out of darkness,"
has shone in our hearts to give the light of the knowledge
of the glory of God in the face of Jesus Christ.

2 Corinthians 4:4-6

5

Rational Gospel, Spiritual Light

The question we are trying to answer (from the previous chapter) is how thinking is involved in the rise of saving faith. This is especially problematic since we have seen how distorted our thinking is by our spiritual blindness. We generally use our minds to justify our desires. And if we are part of the "evil and adulterous generation" because of our sinful nature, how can our thinking be helpfully involved in coming to faith in Christ? To answer this we will try to clarify the nature of faith.

Faith, the Uniquely Receiving Grace

The only kind of faith that matters in the end is saving faith—the faith that unites us to Christ so that his righteousness is counted as ours in *justification*,[1] and his power flows into us for *sanctification*.[2] In other words, at this point I am not interested in faith in general—

---

[1]*Justification* is the biblical teaching that, by grace alone through faith alone, God counts believers in Jesus Christ to be perfectly righteous and totally acceptable in his presence forever. That is, God imputes the perfection of Christ to those who are united to Christ by faith (Rom. 3:28; 4:4–6; 5:1, 18–19; 8:1; 1 Cor. 1:30; 2 Cor. 5:21; Phil. 3:8).

[2]*Sanctification* is the biblical teaching that we are progressively conformed to the image of Christ in our attitudes and words and actions by the power of the Holy Spirit moving through faith to make us become in daily practice what we have already become in Christ (Rom. 6:22; 1 Cor. 5:7; Phil. 2:12–13; 3:12; Eph. 4:24).

the faith of other religions, or the faith of science in the validity of its first principles, or the faith of children in their parents, or any other kind of faith that is not in Christ. I am only interested in the faith that obtains eternal life. The faith that saves (Acts 16:31; Rom. 10:9). The faith that justifies (Rom. 3:28; Gal. 2:16) and sanctifies (Acts 26:18; 1 Pet. 4:11).

To get at the nature of that faith, it is helpful to ponder *why* faith alone justifies. Why not love, or some other virtuous disposition? Here's the way J. Gresham Machen answers this question in his 1925 book *What Is Faith?*

> The true reason why faith is given such an exclusive place by the New Testament, so far as the attainment of salvation is concerned, over against love and over against everything else in man . . . is that faith means *receiving something*, not *doing* something or even *being* some- thing. To say, therefore, that our faith saves us means that we do not save ourselves even in slightest measure, but that God saves us.[3]

In other words, we are justified by faith alone, and not by love, because God intends to make it crystal clear that he does the decisive saving outside of us, and that the person and work of Christ are the sole ground of our acceptance with God.

A hundred years earlier Andrew Fuller (the main rope holder in England for missionary William Carey in India) gave the same explanation:

> Thus it is that justification is ascribed to faith, because it is by faith that we receive Christ; and thus it is by *faith only*, and not by any other grace. Faith is peculiarly a *receiving grace* which none other is. Were we said to be justified by repentance, by love, or by any other grace, it would convey to us the idea of something good in us being the *consid- eration* on which the blessing was bestowed; but justification by faith conveys no such idea.[4]

---

[3] J. Gresham Machen, *What Is Faith?* (1925; repr. Edinburgh: Banner of Truth, 1991), 173, emphasis added.
[4] Andrew Fuller, *The Complete Works of Reverend Andrew Fuller*, vol. 1, ed. Joseph Belcher (Harrisonburg, VA: Sprinkle, 1988), 281. "By faith we receive the benefit; but the benefit arises

So, what sets faith apart from other graces and virtues is that it is "a peculiarly receiving grace." That's why Paul says in Ephesians 2:8, "*By grace* you have been saved *through faith.*" *Grace* from God correlates with *faith* in us (see Rom. 4:16). And the reason is that grace is God's free giving, and faith is our helpless receiving. When God justifies us by faith alone, he has respect not to faith as virtue but faith as a receiving of Christ. So it is the same as saying that not our virtue, but Christ's virtue, is the ground of our justification.[5]

What Does Faith Receive?

Now, the key question is: What does faith receive in order to be justifying faith? The answer, of course, is that faith receives Jesus. "Believe in the Lord Jesus, and you will be saved" (Acts 16:31). "To all who did receive *him,* who *believed* in his name, he gave the right to become children of God" (John 1:12). Faith saves because it receives Jesus.

But we must make clear what this actually means, because there are so many people who say they have received Christ and believed on Christ but give little or no evidence that they are spiritually alive. They are unresponsive to the spiritual beauty of Jesus. They are unmoved by the glories of Christ. They don't have the spirit of the apostle Paul when he said, "I count everything as loss because of the *surpassing worth* of knowing Christ Jesus my Lord. For his sake I have suffered the loss of all things and count them as rubbish, in order that I may *gain Christ*" (Phil. 3:8). This is not their spirit, yet they say they have received Christ. It looks as though it is possible to "receive Christ" and not have him for what he is.

One way to describe this problem is to say that when these people "receive Christ," they do not receive him as *supremely valu-*

---

not from faith, but from Christ. Hence the same thing which is ascribed in some places to faith, is in others ascribed to the obedience, death, and resurrection of Christ" (p. 282).

[5]For a much fuller explanation and defense of this understanding of justification by faith alone, see John Piper, *Counted Righteous in Christ: Should We Abandon the Imputation of Christ's Righteousness?* (Wheaton, IL: Crossway, 2002); John Piper, *The Future of Justification: A Response to N. T. Wright* (Wheaton, IL: Crossway, 2007).

able. They receive him simply as sin-forgiver (because they love being guilt-free), and as rescuer-from-hell (because they love being pain-free), and as healer (because they love being disease-free), and as protector (because they love being safe), and as prosperity-giver (because they love being wealthy), and as creator (because they want a personal universe), and as Lord of history (because they want order and purpose). But they don't receive him as supremely and personally valuable for who he is. They don't receive him the way Paul did when he spoke of "the *surpassing worth* of knowing Christ Jesus my Lord." They don't receive him as he really is—more glorious, more beautiful, more wonderful, more satisfying, than everything else in the universe. They don't prize *him* or treasure *him* or cherish *him* or delight in *him*.

Such a "receiving" of Christ is the kind of receiving an unregenerate, "natural" person can do. This is a "receiving" of Christ that requires no change in human nature. You don't have to be born again to love being guilt-free and pain-free and disease-free and safe and wealthy. All natural men without any spiritual life love these things. But to embrace Jesus as your supreme treasure requires a new nature. No one does this naturally. You must be born again (John 3:3). You must be a new creation in Christ (2 Cor. 5:17; Gal. 6:15). You must be made spiritually alive (Eph. 2:1–4). "No one can say 'Jesus is Lord' [and mean it!] except in the Holy Spirit" (1 Cor. 12:3).

Faith Receives Christ as Savior, Lord, and Supreme Treasure

Therefore, saving faith is a receiving of Christ for who he really is and what he really is, namely, more glorious, more wonderful, more satisfying, and, therefore, more valuable than anything in the universe. Saving faith says, "I receive you as my Savior, my Lord, my supreme Treasure; and I count everything as loss because of the surpassing worth of knowing Christ Jesus my Lord" (see Phil. 3:8).

This is why Jesus said, "Therefore, any one of you who does

not renounce all that he has cannot be my disciple" (Luke 14:33). And again, "Whoever loves father or mother more than me is not worthy of me, and whoever loves son or daughter more than me is not worthy of me" (Matt. 10:37). And, "The kingdom of heaven is like treasure hidden in a field, which a man found and covered up. Then in his joy he goes and sells all that he has and buys that field" (Matt. 13:44).

The infinite glory of Jesus makes him infinitely valuable and infinitely satisfying. Saving faith receives *this* Christ. Not that we experience the fullness of joy now or the climax of satisfaction in this life, but we taste it (Ps. 34:8) and we know where it is found (John 6:35) and we "press on to make it [our] own, because Christ Jesus has made [us] his own" (Phil. 3:12).

The Awakening of the Spiritual Sight of Glory

Now, with this clarification of what faith is, we are in a position to ask how our thinking and God's illumining interact in the awakening of this faith. What we have seen concerning the nature of saving faith determines what will be a sufficient and reasonable ground for such faith and how that ground is known. Saving faith cannot rest only on the ground of raw facts—facts like Jesus is the Messiah, and Christ lived a perfect life, and Christ died for sinners, and Christ is God, and Christ rose from the dead. The Devil believes all those facts (James 2:19).

The nature of saving faith demands more than facts as a ground—not less, but more. We have seen that saving faith is not the mere receiving of facts. It is the receiving of Christ as the one who died for us and rose again, and is infinitely glorious, and wondrously beautiful, and supremely valuable. Therefore, the ground of such faith must be the spiritual sight of such glory and beauty and value.

This sight is not separate from thinking about historical gospel facts. We must hear and understand with our minds the old, old story. But hearing and understanding the facts of the gospel story are not identical with seeing Christ's divine glory in the gospel. Therefore, human reason—the use of the mind to learn and explain and defend the facts of the gospel—plays an *indispensable* but *not the decisive* role in the awakening and establishing of saving faith. We must hear the story and get the gospel facts and the doctrine right. But the decisive ground of saving faith is the glory of Christ seen in the gospel.

The Text That Gives the Ground

Here is the key biblical text where we can see this point:

> The god of this world has blinded the minds of the unbelievers, to keep them from seeing the light of the gospel of the glory of Christ, who is the image of God. For what we proclaim is not ourselves, but Jesus Christ as Lord, with ourselves as your servants for Jesus' sake. For God, who said, "Let light shine out of darkness," has shone in our hearts to give the light of the knowledge of the glory of God in the face of Jesus Christ. (2 Cor. 4:4–6)

Six observations from this text will clarify how human thinking and divine revealing work together in awakening saving faith.

1) The Glory of Christ Is Seen in the Gospel

Verse 4 says that the gospel is the "gospel of the glory of Christ, who is the image of God." This is what must be seen so that saving faith will respond to the gospel and receive Christ for who he really is—infinitely glorious. Jonathan Edwards commented on this text to the same effect. He said, "Nothing can be more evident, than that a saving belief of the gospel is here spoken of . . . as arising from the mind's being enlightened to behold the divine glory of the things it exhibits."[6]

In other words, the ground of saving faith is the glory of Christ seen in the gospel. Don't separate "the divine glory" of Christ from

---

[6]Jonathan Edwards, *Religious Affections*, The Works of Jonathan Edwards, vol. 2, ed. John E. Smith (New Haven, CT: Yale University Press, 1959), 298.

the objective events and facts of the gospel. That is where the glory is revealed. The revelation of the glory of Christ is not a mystical experience cut loose from our thinking about Christ in the gospel. Just as the psalmist can say, "The heavens declare the glory of God," so Paul is saying, "The gospel declares the glory of Christ." If we stop thinking about the gospel, we will not see the glory of Christ. It is the "light *of the gospel* of the glory of Christ."

2) The Glory of Christ Is Really There

This divine glory is really and objectively there in the gospel. Otherwise, Paul would not speak of the god of this world *blinding* the minds of unbelievers. If something is not really there, you don't need to be blind to miss it. But if it is really there, you must be blind to miss it. Therefore, "the light of the gospel of the glory of Christ" is really there. It is a self-authenticating divine glory. Edwards calls it an "ineffable, distinguishing, evidential excellency in the gospel."[7]

Saving faith is "reasonable" in the sense that there are real reasons to support it. It is not based on a figment of the imagination. Its basis is the glory of Christ in the gospel. It is a real gospel and a real glory.

3) The Glory of Christ Is Seen through the Facts of the Gospel

Verse 5 clarifies and confirms what we have already seen in the first observation. The sight of this "distinguishing, evidential excellency"—the glory of Christ in the gospel—is not seen in a vision or a dream or a whispered word from the Holy Spirit. It is seen in the biblical story of Christ as the inspired apostle preaches the gospel of Christ. Verse 5: "What we proclaim is not ourselves, but Jesus Christ as Lord, with ourselves as your servants for Jesus' sake."

Here is the place of thinking and reason. Paul uses his mind to

[7] Ibid., 300.

proclaim and explain and defend and confirm the facts of the gospel. And we use our mind to hear it and construe its meaning and weigh its claims. Paul argues that Jesus is the Christ and that he rose from the dead and that he died for our sins.[8] Paul reasons with facts and arguments and sets Christ forth. Therefore, we know that the sight of the self-authenticating glory of Christ is not separate from the rational presentation and demonstration and reception of the truth of the gospel. That rational presentation and reception—the work of the mind—is indispensable.

4) The Decisive Ground of Saving Faith Is God's Gift of Sight to the Eyes of the Heart

At this point we can see how the nature of saving faith and the ground of saving faith fit together. The glory of Christ in the gospel is the decisive ground of saving faith because saving faith is the receiving of Christ as infinitely glorious and supremely valuable.[9] Or to turn it around: since saving faith is a receiving of Christ as our highest treasure, therefore the ground of that faith is the spiritual sight of Christ as supremely beautiful and valuable. Verse 6 describes how this sight of Christ happens even though we are by nature blind and resistant.

Seeing this compelling spiritual light is a gift of God. This is the point of verse 6: "God, who said, 'Let light shine out of darkness,' has shone in our hearts to give the light of the knowledge of the glory of God in the face of Jesus Christ." Decisive in our seeing is God's causing light to shine in our hearts.

According to verse 4, we could not see this "light of the gospel of the glory of Christ who is the image of God" because we were blinded by the god of this world. No amount of reasoning or his-

---

[8]For examples of Paul's arguing see Acts 17:2, 4, 17; 18:4, 19; 19:8, 9; 20:7, 9; 24:25.

[9]"Thus a soul may have a kind of intuitive knowledge of the divinity of the things exhibited in the gospel; not that he judges the doctrines of the gospel to be from God, without any argument or deduction at all; but it is without any long chain of arguments; the argument is but one, and the evidence direct; the mind ascends to the truth of the gospel but by one step, and that is its divine glory." Edwards, *Religious Affections*, 298–99.

torical argument alone can produce spiritual sight in the blind. This is the limit of thinking. Nevertheless, the rational proclamation and comprehension of the gospel facts are indispensable. "We proclaim . . . Jesus Christ as Lord" (v. 5).

But now, in verse 6, the decisive change happens. God opens the eyes of our heart. The gospel of Christ crucified and risen (and rationally set forth in preaching and teaching) becomes radiant with "ineffable, distinguishing, evidential excellency"—with "the glory of God in the face of Jesus Christ." This means that our hearts are changed. Spiritual death is replaced with spiritual life (Eph. 2:5); spiritual blindness is replaced with spiritual sight (v. 4 contrasted with v. 6).

Because our hearts now see Christ as infinitely valuable, our resistance to the truth is overcome. Our thinking is no longer the slave of deceitful desires, because our desires are changed. Christ is now the supreme treasure. So our thinking is made docile to the truth of the gospel. We don't use our thinking to distort the gospel anymore. We don't call it foolish. We call it wisdom and power and glory (1 Cor. 1:23–24).

What is being described here in 2 Corinthians 4:6 is the same as the new birth.[10] The change is profound. It is the key to the question we raised earlier: How can such a darkened, sinful heart produce a way of thinking that gives rise to saving faith? The answer is that God's illumination and regeneration produce a profound change in the way the heart perceives reality.

Thinking back to chapter 4, this means that we now see the glory of our bridegroom as more precious than anything else (Matt. 9:15; 25:1). Our adulterous desires (Matt. 16:4) for other satisfactions have been crucified with him (Gal. 2:20; Col. 3:3–5). And our hearts are transformed and brought into harmony with the truth of

---

[10]For the relationship between God's illumination of our hearts and the biblical teaching on the new birth see John Piper, *Finally Alive: What Happens When We Are Born Again* (Fearn, Ross-shire, UK: Christian Focus, 2009), 119, 178.

Christ's worth. This is why our thinking can now stand in the service of the gospel and become the humble agent of saving faith.

5) Saving Faith Is Reasonable

This ground of faith is a reasonable ground, and the conviction that flows from it is a reasonable conviction. It goes beyond what mere thinking and reasoning upon the facts can produce, but it is itself reasonable. Jonathan Edwards explains, "By a reasonable conviction, I mean, a conviction founded on real evidence, or upon that which is a good reason, or just ground of conviction."[11] Nothing is more reasonable than that saving faith, as the receiving of Christ as infinitely glorious, must be grounded on the spiritual sight of his divine glory.[12]

6) This Is the Only Path to Spiritual Certainty

The reason this understanding of the interworking of human thinking and divine illumination is so important is that the great mass of ordinary people (and I count myself in this number) cannot come to an unshakable conviction about the truth of Christianity any other way. If our only confidence rests on rational historical and philosophical argumentation, most people will not have the time or the resources or the training to carry through such extended reasoning. And even those who devote themselves to this task know only probabilities, but not spiritual certainty. But the apostle John said, "I write these things to you who believe in the name of the Son of God that you may *know* that you have eternal life" (1 John 5:13). We are meant to *know* that the gospel is true and that we are saved, not cross our fingers.

Jonathan Edwards had a brilliant mind. No one could out-argue Edwards. But what drove him at this point was his burden for the Houssatunnuck Indians near where he lived in New England in

---

[11]Edwards, *Religious Affections*, 295.
[12]"There is no spiritual conviction of the judgment, but what arises from an apprehension of the spiritual beauty and glory of divine things." Ibid., 307.

the eighteenth century. How could they come to a firm and reasonable faith in Christ? The same concern moves me: not only how to commend and defend Christianity to intellectuals, but how to proclaim it among my ordinary neighbors and among thousands of unreached peoples around the world who cannot wait for generations of education. Here is the way Edwards described his burden:

> Unless men may come to a reasonable, solid persuasion and conviction of the truth of the gospel, by the internal evidences of it . . . by a sight of its glory; it is impossible that those who are illiterate, and unacquainted with history, should have any thorough and effectual conviction of it at all. They may without this, see a great deal of probability of it; it may be reasonable for them to give much credit to what learned men and historians tell them. . . . But to have a conviction, so clear, and evident, and assuring, as to be sufficient to induce them, with boldness to sell all, confidently and fearlessly to run the venture of the loss of all things, and of enduring the most exquisite and long continued torments, and to trample the world under foot, and count all things but dung for Christ, the evidence they can have from history, cannot be sufficient.[13]

Yes, and that is the kind of Christian I want to awaken. Fearless, venturing the loss of everything, ready to endure the worst hardships for Christ, trampling the Devil underfoot, and counting everything dung for Christ's sake; and when death comes in this cause, to call it gain.

So I conclude that we must use our minds and we must know that the use of our minds is not enough. We must exercise our reason in the proclamation and explanation and confirmation and comprehension of the gospel. We must contend for the faith once delivered to the saints (Jude 3). We must be ready, like Paul, to go to prison for "the defense and confirmation of the gospel" (Phil. 1:7). That is indispensable.

---

[13]Ibid., 303. "Miserable is the condition of the Houssatunnuck Indians, and others, who have lately manifested a desire to be instructed in Christianity, if they can come at no evidence of the truth of Christianity, sufficient to induce them to sell all for Christ, in any other way but this" (p. 304).

But as we use all our renewed mental powers for Christ, we must pray with Paul that the Holy Spirit would attend the preaching and hearing of the gospel. We must pray that the God who said, "Let light shine out of darkness," would shine in our hearts to give the light of the knowledge of the glory of God in the face of Jesus Christ. Only when that happens will true faith be awakened and true Christians be created who say, "I count everything as loss because of the surpassing worth of knowing Christ Jesus my Lord" (Phil. 3:8).

Turning Now from Conversion to the First Commandment

Having clarified the role of thinking in how we come to faith in Christ (chapters 4 and 5), we turn now in chapter 6 to the role of thinking in how we fulfill the Great Commandment—to love God. Jesus said that we should love God with all our minds (Matt. 22:37). Some have treated this as if it means "think hard and think accurately, and that act of thinking *is* loving God." But I doubt that.

I will suggest that loving God with the mind means that *our thinking is wholly engaged to do all it can to awaken and express the heartfelt fullness of treasuring God above all things.* Treasuring God is the essence of loving him, and the mind serves this love by comprehending (imperfectly and partially, but truly) the truth and beauty and worth of the Treasure. We can't love God without knowing God. And Jesus is the fullest revelation of God. If we know him truly, we know God. And the Bible is our only reliable access to knowing Jesus truly. Therefore, we see again the vital place of reading—that is, thinking (chapter 3)—in knowing and loving God. What is the biblical basis for this understanding of loving God with our minds? That's what we turn to now.

Clarifying the Meaning of Loving God

And one of them, a lawyer, asked him a question to test him.
"Teacher, which is the great commandment in the Law?"
And he said to him, "You shall love the Lord your God
with all your heart and with all your soul and with all your mind.
This is the great and first commandment.
And a second is like it: You shall love your neighbor as yourself.
On these two commandments depend all the Law
and the Prophets."

Matthew 22:35-40

6

Love for God:
Treasuring God with
All Your Mind

A Pharisee asked Jesus, "Teacher, which is the great commandment in the Law?" He answered, "You shall love the Lord your God with all your heart and with all your soul and with all your mind. This is the great and first commandment. And a second is like it: You shall love your neighbor as yourself" (Matt. 22:36–39). Therefore, the greatest commandment in the Bible is to love God. And Jesus says to do this not only with our heart and soul but also with our mind.

What Does It Mean to Love God with Your Mind?

What does it mean to love God "with all your mind"? I take it to mean that we direct our thinking in a certain way; namely, *our thinking should be wholly engaged to do all it can to awaken and express the heartfelt fullness of treasuring God above all things.*

Let me unpack that with four brief statements, and then I will argue for it from the words of Jesus.

Notice, first, that I speak of the activity of the mind as "thinking." So to love God with the mind is to love him in the way we use our mind to think.

Second, notice that I construe the word "all" in the phrase, "Love God with *all* your mind," as referring to the full engagement of the mind: "Our thinking should be *wholly* engaged . . . "

Third, I define loving God mainly as treasuring God. That is, it is an experience of cherishing, delighting, admiring, and valuing. It's the sort of thing Paul was expressing for Jesus when he said, "I count everything as loss because of the surpassing worth of knowing Christ Jesus my Lord" (Phil. 3:8). Love for God is an affair of the affections. Ideas and thoughts and thinking are crucial (as we will see) but they are not what love *is*.

And fourth, I do not say that thinking is identical with loving. I say that thinking functions to "awaken" and "express" love. One of the reasons for this is that the Devil can *think* true thoughts about God. But such thinking would not be love. For thinking to be loving, it must be more than thinking.

With that summary in view, now let's turn to the argument.

The Meaning of Heart, Soul, and Mind

What do the terms *heart*, *soul*, and *mind* refer to? What is plain from the Bible is that they overlap in meaning. Nevertheless, they do have different focuses. Concerning *heart* and *mind*, consider that the one other place in the four Gospels where the word *mind* (*dianoia*) occurs, other than in the command to love God, is Luke 1:51. There it is translated "thoughts," and these thoughts are happening, surprisingly, in the "heart." "He has scattered the proud in the *thoughts* [*dianoia*] *of their hearts*." So *mind* and *heart* overlap. The heart has its thoughts and the mind has its "spirit" or, you might say, its "heart," as Paul says in Ephesians 4:23: "Be renewed in the *spirit of your minds*." Nevertheless, the mind and heart are not identical.

Concerning the meaning of the soul, consider that Jesus said,

"Do not fear those who kill the body but cannot kill the *soul*. Rather fear him who can destroy both *soul* and body in hell" (Matt. 10:28). This implies that *soul* is the fullness of life or personhood apart from the body. The body can be killed and yet the soul still live. Therefore, the soul includes the heart and the mind, since Jesus says that though the body may perish, the soul is rescued, which would surely include the rescue of the heart and the mind as part of the soul.

What then shall we say about these terms? We may summarize like this: *heart* highlights the center of our volitional and emotional life without excluding thought (Luke 1:51). *Soul* highlights our human life as a whole ("man became a living creature," Gen. 2:7), though sometimes distinguished from the body (Matt. 10:28). *Mind* highlights our thinking capacity. And when the term *strength* is added, as in Mark 12:30, it highlights the capacity to make vigorous efforts both bodily and mentally (Mark 5:4; Luke 21:36).

So taken together the point is that we are to treasure God with all that we are. There is no part of us that should be uninvolved in treasuring God above all things. And the repeated word "all" (love him "with *all* your heart and with *all* your soul and with *all* your mind") means that not just every faculty should be engaged in treasuring God, but they should be *fully* engaged. The degree of our valuing God should be to the highest degree. Extensively (with *every* faculty) and intensively (with the *whole* faculty) we are to treasure God above all things.

So I take the word "mind" in Matthew 22:37 to refer to that aspect of our being especially devoted to *thinking*. Loving God with all our mind means wholly engaging our thinking to do all it can to awaken and express the heartfelt fullness of treasuring God above all things.

Loving God Is Treasuring God: Slight Pointers and Solid Reasons

Now, why do I define loving God mainly as treasuring God? Why do I believe that love for God is most essentially an experience of the affections, not mere thought or mere behavior? There are slight pointers, then solid reasons.

Slight Pointers

One of the slight pointers is that according to the *order* of words in Jesus' command, the heart is mentioned first: "You shall love the Lord your God with all your *heart* and with all your soul and with all your mind." This may suggest that the deepest source of love to God is the heart, which then comes to expression through acts of the soul and the mind.

Another slight pointer is that when Luke records the Great Commandment, the preposition he uses with "heart" is different from the other three. "You shall love the Lord your God *with* [*ex*] all your heart and with [*en*] all your soul and with [*en*] all your strength and with [*en*] all your mind" (Luke 10:27). It doesn't come through in English, but the preposition connected to "heart" (*ex*) suggests that the heart is the source of our love for God, while the preposition (*en*) used with soul, strength, and mind suggests that they are instruments of that love. This is a slight pointer—suggestive, not determinative—to the fact that love is primarily an affection of the heart.

Another pointer is that Moses promised in Deuteronomy 30:6 that someday love for God would be possible in a new way because God would circumcise the *heart*. "The LORD your God will circumcise your heart and the heart of your offspring, so that you will love the LORD your God with all your heart and with all your soul, that you may live." The focus is on the change that is needed in *the heart* so that love for God can come into being. And then it gets expressed "with all your soul that you may live." This promise was fulfilled in Jesus because he died for our sins and changes our heart so that it can see God as compellingly beautiful (Matt. 11:27; John 17:26).

Solid Reasons

I use the phrase "compellingly beautiful" to shift our focus from slight pointers to solid reasons. The phrase stresses two things that

I am arguing for. One is that loving God is not a mere decision. You cannot merely decide to love classical music—or country western music—much less God. The music must become compelling. Something must change inside of you. That change makes possible the awakening of a compelling sense of its attractiveness. So it is with God. You do not merely decide to love him. Something changes inside of you, and as a result he becomes compellingly attractive. His glory—his beauty—compels your admiration and delight. He becomes your supreme treasure. You love him.

The other thing I am emphasizing in the phrase "compellingly beautiful" is that love for God is not essentially thought or behavior but affection—not ideas or deeds but delight. God is our supreme pleasure. We prefer above all else to know him and see him and be with him and be like him. There are solid reasons for believing that love for God is most essentially an experience of the affections, not mere thoughts or behaviors.

The Second Commandment Is like the First

First, Jesus distinguished between the first and second commandments. He said, "You shall love the Lord your God with all your heart and with all your soul and with all your mind. This is the great and first commandment. And a second is like it: You shall love your neighbor as yourself" (Matt. 22:37–39). The second is like the first. It is not the same as the first. It is not the first, in other words. Loving God is not defined as loving our neighbor. They are different. The first is primary and depends on no greater obedience. The second is secondary and depends on the first—on loving God.

To be sure, they are not separated, because true love for God will bring about love for people. But they are different. This means that the thoughts and behaviors of love toward others are not identical with loving God. They are the *overflow* or fruit of loving God. Loving God is not synonymous with the way we treat others. It is a compelling admiration for, and allegiance to, and delight in God.

True Worship Is from the Heart

Second, Jesus said to the Pharisees when they criticized the freedom of his disciples, "Well did Isaiah prophesy of you hypocrites, as it is written, 'This people honors me with their lips, but their heart is far from me; in vain do they worship me'" (Mark 7:6–7). In other words, Jesus says that external actions—even religious ones directed toward him—are not the essence of worship. They are not the essence of love. What happens in the heart is essential. The external behaviors will be pleasing to God when they flow from a heart that freely treasures God above all things.

The Opposite, Hate, Is Not a Thought

Third, Jesus said, "No one can serve two masters, for either he will hate the one and love the other, or he will be devoted to the one and despise the other. You cannot serve God and money" (Matt. 6:24). The opposite of loving God is "hating" and "despising." These are strong emotional words. They imply that the positive counterpart is also a strong emotion. So loving God is a strong inward emotion, not a mere outward action.

But someone might say that "serve" is the key word in Matthew 6:24 and implies that love for God is serving God. But that is not what it says. It says that the reason you cannot serve two masters (God and money) is that behind the behaviors of serving are two diametrically opposed passions: hate versus love, and devotion versus despising. Jesus does not equate loving God with serving God. He roots serving God in loving God. Loving God is treasuring him the way people do money, only vastly more and for different reasons.

Loving God is most essentially treasuring God—valuing him, cherishing him, admiring him, desiring him. And loving him with all our mind means that *our thinking is wholly engaged to do all it can to awaken and express this heartfelt fullness of treasuring God above all things.*

God, the Gladness of All My Joys

This way of seeing love for God is confirmed by the way God is loved in the Psalms. Since Jesus saw himself as the goal and focus and fulfillment of the Psalms (Matt. 5:17; Luke 24:27; John 5:39), we would expect him to demand a love that extends and fulfills what the psalmists experienced. In the Psalms we read of love to God that is absolutely exclusive: "Whom have I in heaven but you? And there is nothing on earth that I desire besides you" (Ps. 73:25). "I say to the LORD, 'You are my Lord; I have no good apart from you'" (Ps. 16:2).

What can this exclusivity possibly mean, since the psalmists also speak, for example, of loving other people (Ps. 16:3)? We get a clue in Psalm 43:4 where the psalmist says, "I will go to the altar of God, to *God my exceeding joy*." This last phrase ("my exceeding joy") is literally, "the gladness of my rejoicing" or "the joy of my exultation."[1] This points to God as the joy of all our joys.

In other words, in all my rejoicing over all the good things that God has made, God himself is the heart of my joy, the gladness of my joy. In all my rejoicing in everything, there is a central rejoicing in God. Every joy that does not have God as its central gladness is a hollow joy and in the end will burst like a bubble. This is what led Augustine to pray, "He loves thee too little who loves anything together with Thee, which he loves not for thy sake."[2]

Sibi Mutuo Causae

Finally, from the summary I gave at the beginning of this chapter, one other thing needs clarifying. I said that the way thinking relates to loving God is to "awaken" and "express" love. The fires of love for God need fuel. And the fires of love for God drive the engines of thought and deed. There is a circle. Thinking feeds the fire, and the fire fuels more thinking and doing. I love God because I know him. And I want to know him more because I love him.

---

[1] The Hebrew phrase is two words for joy or rejoicing: שִׂמְחַת גִּילִי.
[2] Augustine, *Confessions*, bk. 10, chap. 29.

Thomas Goodwin (1600–1679), one of the English Puritan pastors and, for a time, president of Magdalen College, Oxford, expressed this wonderful mutual benefit of serious thinking and spiritual affections:

> Indeed, thoughts and affections are *sibi mutuo causae*—the mutual causes of each other: "Whilst I mused, the fire burned" (Psalm 39:3); so that thoughts are the bellows that kindle and inflame affections; and then if they are inflamed, they cause thoughts to boil; therefore men newly converted to God, having new and strong affections, can with more pleasure think of God than any.[3]

Knowing God Is the Root of Loving God

The main reason that thinking and loving are connected is that we cannot love God without knowing God; and the way we know God is by the Spirit-enabled use of our minds. So to "love God with all your mind" means engaging all your powers of thought to know God as fully as possible in order to treasure him for all he is worth.

God is not honored by groundless love. In fact, there is no such thing. If we do not know anything about God, there is nothing in our mind to awaken love. If love does not come from knowing God, there is no point calling it love *for God*. There may be some vague attraction in our heart or some unfocused gratitude in our soul, but if they do not arise from knowing God, they are not love for God.

If Jesus Is Not Worshiped, God Is Not Loved

Jesus is the fullest revelation of God. "Whoever has seen me," he said, "has seen the Father" (John 14:9). This means that knowing and loving Jesus is the test of knowing and loving God. So Jesus said, "I know that you do not have the love of God within you. I have come in my Father's name, and you do not receive me" (John 5:42–43).

---

[3]Thomas Goodwin, "The Vanity of Thoughts," in *The Works of Thomas Goodwin*, 12 vols. (Eureka, CA: Tanski Publications), 3:526–27.

His adversaries "do not have the love of God within [them]" because they do not receive him. "The one who rejects me rejects him who sent me" (Luke 10:16). If they loved God, they would love Jesus. Why? Because he makes God known more clearly and more fully than any other revelation.

Therefore, the main reason Jesus says to love God *with all our mind* is that the mind is the faculty for thinking about Jesus, and therefore about God. If we did not use our minds to know and think about the fullest revelation of God in the person and work of Jesus, we would not know God. And if we did not know him, we would not love him. And if we did not love him, we would not express his worth in all the other uses of our mind.

Therefore, God has given us minds so that, by thinking with the Spirit's help, we can know the truth and beauty and worth of God through Jesus and treasure him above all things and spend our lives expressing this in as many ways as our minds can pursue. Or, as I said at the beginning of this chapter, loving God with all our mind means that *our thinking is wholly engaged to do all it can to awaken and express the heartfelt fullness of treasuring God above all things.*

But If Relativism Holds, All Is Vain

But everything I have said so far is pointless if knowing is impossible or if nothing is there to know. My aim to invigorate you in the pursuit of knowing God for the sake of loving God would be in vain if there were no such thing as reliable, objective knowledge of real things. But one of the most common notions today is that such knowledge is impossible.

One of the names for this attitude is *relativism*. In the next two chapters, I will try to explain what it is and what Jesus thought about it. I will argue in chapter 7 that relativism is neither intellectually compelling nor morally upright. It is emotionally gratifying because it seems to protect my personal preferences from external judgment. Jesus knew this sort of evasive use of the mind. He did not like it.

Then in chapter 8, I will try to build up your immune system against the intellectual virus of relativism by inoculating you, if you're willing, with seven harmful and immoral aspects of the disease.

Facing the Challenge
of Relativism

And when he entered the temple,
the chief priests and the elders of the people
came up to [Jesus] as he was teaching, and said,
"By what authority are you doing these things, and
who gave you this authority?" Jesus answered them,
"I also will ask you one question, and if you tell me the
answer, then I also will tell you by what authority I do these
things. The baptism of John, from where did it come?
From heaven or from man?" And they discussed it among
themselves, saying, "If we say, 'From heaven,' he will say to us,
'Why then did you not believe him?' But if we say, 'From man,'
we are afraid of the crowd, for they all hold that John was
a prophet." So they answered Jesus, "We do not know."
And he said to them, "Neither will I tell you by
what authority I do these things."

Matthew 21:23-27

7

Jesus Meets the Relativists

Implicit in the previous chapters is the assumption that God and his ways are knowable—not perfectly or comprehensively in this life (1 Cor. 13:12), but truly (John 14:9). Thinking is not just entertainment on the stage of life where nothing is real. It is really useful in knowing the God who is really there. It is useful in knowing what God has revealed about himself and about this world and how we should live in it. And we saw in chapter 5 how God has designed it to be effective in knowing the glory of Christ in the gospel, which means that thinking is essential in coming to faith in Christ and receiving forgiveness for our sins and the gift of eternal life.

Relativism and Truth

But there have always been people who use their minds another way. Some claim there is no objective, knowable reality outside ourselves. They say that our thinking does not produce reliable knowledge of God or anything else outside of us. Instead our observations and our thinking simply give rise to expressions of personal or communal preferences and perspectives. So thinking does not lead us to universally valid truth or beauty or goodness defined by the nature and will of God. It simply leads us to expressions of what we feel and perceive. But those expressions do not correspond to universally valid truth outside ourselves.

One name for this way of viewing the world is *relativism*. In this view, *truth*, if the word is used at all, does not refer to universally true statements about God and man and life. It may refer to your own inner integrity—acting in accord with the world as you see it. But it doesn't refer to truth that all people should agree with. If this truth-denying viewpoint is true (there are problems even stating the problem), then I should not be writing this book the way I am.

Why the Issue of Relativism Matters

My goal is to encourage you to make serious thinking an important part of the way you pursue the knowledge of God. This goal is based on the conviction that God exists and that he has revealed himself and his will mainly in Jesus Christ through the Bible, but also in his world. God *is* ultimate Truth. And he never changes. Therefore, he is a firm, universal, never-changing foundation for truth about man and the world and life. Who God is and what he says is truth. My goal is to encourage you to embrace the work of thinking as a means of knowing this truth.

This goal would be pointless if such truth did not exist or were not knowable. So relativism of this kind is obviously something I think is wrong and, indeed, very harmful. So what I would like to do in this chapter, and the next one, is examine what relativism is and what Jesus thought about it, and why it is, in fact, deeply evil.

Right Relativistic Thinking

Let's start by agreeing that there is such a thing as knowledge that is relative. In fact, let's go farther and say that thinking this way—thinking relatively—is not only good but indispensable.

For example, if I say Barack Obama is tall, that statement may be true or false in relation to—that is, "relative" to—different standards of measurement. "Barack Obama is tall" would be true in relation to me. But the statement "Barack Obama is tall" would be false in relation to the Sears Tower or giraffes. So we say that the statement "Barack Obama is tall" is true or false "relative" to the standard of measurement being used at the time.

This is a good and indispensable way of thinking and speaking. If you are unable to speak of truth-claims being relative in this sense, you may accuse people of error who have in fact spoken truth because you have not clarified the context or the standard they are using for measuring the truth of the statement.

Many examples from our daily speech could be given. *My father was old when he passed away.* That's true relative to men. But it's false relative to civilizations or Redwood trees. *That car was speeding.* True, relative to the 35-mile-per-hour speed limit. False, relative to a NASCAR race. *That baby's cry is loud.* True, relative to ordinary human conversation. False, relative to a thunderclap. And so on.

The reason we do not call this way of thinking *relativism* is that we are assuming that the one who says Barack Obama is tall and the one who says he is short both believe there is an objective, external standard for validating the statement as true. For one person, the standard is human beings, and for the other, it may be giraffes. So as soon as the two people know what standard the other is using, they can agree with each other, or they can argue on the basis of the same standard. These arguments are not because of relativism. In fact, these arguments are possible only because relativism is rejected by the arguers.

What Is Relativism?

So then what is the relative way of thinking that we ordinarily call *relativism*? We are dealing with relativism if a person says one of these four things:

• There is no objective, external standard for measuring the truth or falsehood of a statement.

• There may be an external standard, but we can't know if there is.

• There is an objective standard; we know it is there, but no one can figure out what it means, so it can't function as a universally valid standard.

• There may be an external, objective standard, but I don't care what it is. I'm not going to submit to it. I'm not going to base my convictions on it. I will create my own standards.

Such statements may sound silly as long as we are talking about Barack Obama's height. So let's shift over to something explosive, controversial, and immediately relevant. Consider the statement "Sexual relations between two males is wrong." Two people may disagree on this and not be relativists. They may both say, "There is an objective, external standard for assessing this statement, namely, God's will revealed in the inspired Christian Bible." One may say the Bible teaches that this is wrong, and the other may say that the Bible permits it. This would not be relativism.

Relativism comes into play when someone says, "There is no knowable, objective, external standard for right and wrong that is valid for everyone. And so your statement that sexual relations between two males is wrong is relative to *your* standard of measurement, but you can't claim that others should submit to that standard of assessment." This is the essence of relativism: no one standard of true and false, right and wrong, good and bad, or beautiful and ugly, can preempt any other standard. No standard is valid for everyone.

The Essence of Relativism

What does this imply about truth? Relativists may infer from this that there is no such thing as truth. It is simply an unhelpful and confusing category since there are no external, objective standards that are valid for everyone. Or they may continue to use the word *truth* but simply mean by it *what conforms to your subjective preferences*. You may prefer the Bible or the Koran or the Book of Mormon or Mao's *Little Red Book* or the sayings of Confucius or the philosophy of Ayn Rand or your own immediate desires or any of a hundred other standards. In that case, you will hear the language of "true for you, but not true for me." In either case, we are dealing with relativism.

In sum, then, the essence of relativism is the conviction that truth-claims—like "sexual relations between two males is wrong"—are not based on standards of assessment that are valid for everyone. There are no such standards that we can know. Concepts like true and false, right and wrong, good and bad, beautiful and ugly, are useful for expressing personal preferences or agreed-upon community values, but they have no claim to be based on a universally valid standard.

Jesus Meets the Relativists

What shall we make of this? Why have I assumed this is a bad way to see the world? Let's begin our assessment of relativism with an interaction between Jesus and some classic practical relativists—not self-conscious, full-blown relativists, just de facto relativists, which are the most common kind, prevalent in every age, not just this one. It will be helpful to watch Jesus meet the relativists. Consider Matthew 21:23–27:

> And when he entered the temple, the chief priests and the elders of the people came up to [Jesus] as he was teaching, and said, "By what authority are you doing these things, and who gave you this authority?" Jesus answered them, "I also will ask you one question, and if you tell me the answer, then I also will tell you by what authority I do these things. The baptism of John, from where did it come? From heaven or from man?" And they discussed it among themselves, saying, "If we say, 'From heaven,' he will say to us, 'Why then did you not believe him?' But if we say, 'From man,' we are afraid of the crowd, for they all hold that John was a prophet." So they answered Jesus, "We do not know." And he said to them, "Neither will I tell you by what authority I do these things."

Look carefully at how the chief priests and elders deal with truth. Jesus asks them to take a stand on a simple truth-claim: either John's baptism is from heaven or from man. Declare what you believe to be the truth.

So they ponder: "If we say that John's baptism is from heaven, then we will be shamed because Jesus will show that we are hypocrites. He'll ask why we haven't believed in John's message. He'll point out that we *say* we think his baptism is from heaven, but we don't *live* like it. We will be shamed before the crowds.

"But if we say that John's baptism is from man, we may be harmed by the crowd, because they all believe he was a prophet. There could be some mob violence against us. Therefore, since we don't want to be shamed, and we don't want to be harmed by a mob, let's not say that either of these options is true. We will simply say that we don't know the answer."

What are we to make of this? This is not full-blown relativism. Rather, what we see here are the seeds of relativism. Here is the way the depraved mind works. Let's make the connection with chapters 4 and 5 on the role of thinking in the rise of faith. What we saw there was that the human mind, apart from transforming grace (Rom. 12:2; Eph. 4:23), is depraved (1 Tim. 6:5) and debased (Rom. 1:28) and hard (2 Cor. 4:4) and darkened and futile (Eph. 4:17–18). But it was created by God to discover the truth and respond to the truth in trusting God and loving people.

But Matthew 21:23–27 is a picture of what has become of the human mind taken captive by sin. The elders and chief priests do not use their minds to formulate a true answer to Jesus' question. How do they use their minds? Oh, they use them carefully. What we see here is not people who should be using their minds in the service of truth but don't use them at all. No. They use them incisively, and Matthew lets us see the inner workings of such thinking. Everybody thinks. The difference is whether we think in service of the truth or in the way the chief priests and the elders think.

Careful Reasoning to Hide the Truth

They reason carefully: "If we say such and such, then such and such will happen. And if we say the other, then something else will happen." They are reasoning carefully. Why? Because the truth is at stake? No, because their ego and their skin are at stake. They don't want to be shamed, and they don't want to be harmed.

This is what we saw in chapter 4. People could draw true inferences from morning and evening skies but would not use that same reasoning process to discern who Jesus was (Matt. 16:1–4). They wanted safety on the seas. But they did not want to know Jesus for who he was. So their minds drew true conclusions from the weather because their skin was at stake. They loved their physical safety. But they claimed to have too little evidence to know the Son of God. He was too threatening to their desires.

So what has become of the mind and its handmaid, language, here in Matthew 21:23–27? The mind has become the nimble, dodging slave of the priests' and elders' passions. And language does the tricky work of covering up the corruption. Truth is irrelevant here in guiding what they say. It doesn't matter whether John's baptism is from heaven or from man. Truth does not matter. What matters is that we not be shamed and that we not be harmed. So we will use language to cover our indifference to truth and our allegiance to the gods of pride and comfort; and we will say, "We do not know."

This Conversation Is Over

Jesus' response is explosively relevant for how we deal with such duplicity. He says, "Neither will I tell you by what authority I do these things." In other words, "This conversation is over. I don't have serious conversations with people like you." Jesus abominates that kind of arrogant, cowardly prostituting of the glorious gifts of human thinking and human language.

I said above that this passage reveals the *seeds* of relativism. What I mean is this: one seed of relativism is the deep, sinful human desire not to be ruled by God or by any standard claiming the authority of God. This deep-seated rebellion can express itself in many ways. One is simply to say: "God, I don't bow to your standards. I create my own." Another more subtle and more common way to rebel is to say: "God's standards don't exist." Or: "God's standards can't be known. That is, there is no universally valid standard for judging my behavior. Therefore, I am free from authority outside myself. I can do as I please." These are the seeds of relativism. This is where it comes from.

No One Is a Relativist at the Bank

Relativism is not a coherent philosophical system. It is riddled with contradictions—both logical and experiential. Sophomores in college know that something is fishy when someone claims the statement to be true that all truths are relative. They may not be able to name the law of non-contradiction, but they are wired with it, and they can smell it in the wind. Claiming truth for a statement that nullifies truth is self-contradictory. But if you are not claiming your defense of relativism is true, why do you expect me to listen?

And every businessman knows that philosophical relativists park their relativism at the door when they go into the bank and read the language of the contract they are about to sign. People don't embrace relativism because it is philosophically satisfying. They embrace it because it is physically and emotionally gratifying. It provides the cover they need at key moments in their lives to do what they want without intrusion from absolutes.

That's what we see in the chief priests and the elders. They don't care about truth. They care about their skin. Therefore, they take the God-given handmaidens of truth—thinking and speaking—and prostitute them as slaves of self-protection. They think their way to an escape and then use language to avoid shame and harm. Self-aggrandizement is the deepest root of relativism.

It is an enemy of the noble use of the mind. It is something we should avoid and grieve over and labor to overcome. One of the ways that we might make some headway in protecting ourselves and following generations from embracing relativism is by pointing out how evil and destructive its effects are. That's where we will turn in the next chapter.

It makes very little difference how much or how little
of the creeds of the Church the Modernist preacher
affirms. . . . He might affirm every jot and tittle of the
Westminster Confession, for example, and yet be separated
by a great gulf from the Reformed Faith.
It is not that part is denied and the rest affirmed;
but all is denied, because all is affirmed merely as useful
or symbolic and not as true.

J. Gresham Machen

The Immorality of Relativism

My goal in this book is to invigorate you for the effort of thinking in the pursuit of God. Relativism, as we saw in the previous chapter, undermines that effort. It kidnaps the happy handmaiden of truth and makes her serve the pride and pleasure of pragmatists. Relativists don't pursue truth. They make the denial of truth serve them. So what I will try to do in this chapter is build up your antibodies against relativism by describing seven harmful and immoral things about it. I am building on the definitions and explanations of chapter 7.

1) Relativism Commits Treason

Relativism is a revolt against the objective reality of God. The sheer existence of God creates the possibility of truth. God is the ultimate and final standard for all claims to truth—who he is, what he wills, and what he says is the external, objective standard for measuring all things. When relativism says that there is no universally valid standard of truth and falsehood, it speaks like an atheist. It commits treason against God.

In James 2:10–11 we see the dynamics of treason in relation

to God's law: "Whoever keeps the whole law but fails in one point has become accountable for all of it." Why? "For he who said, 'Do not commit adultery,' also said, 'Do not murder.'" The key to James's argument here is that he connects our relation to God's law with our relation to God himself. The reason your failure in one point makes you guilty of all is that the same God gave all the law—and what matters is that in rebelling against the law you are rebelling against him.

Relativism is a pervasive rebellion against the very concept of divine law. Therefore, it is a profound rebellion against God. It is a treason that is worse than outright revolt, because it is devious. Instead of saying to God's face, "Your word is false," it says to man, "There is no such thing as a universally binding divine word." This is treason against the King of the universe.

Oh, how thankful we should be that the King has declared an amnesty for the whole world of traitors. We were all once in that kind of rebellion against his truth and beauty. But he sent his Son to purchase this amnesty with his life and proclaim it with his word. He said, "The Son of Man came not to be served but to serve, and to give his life as a ransom for many" (Mark 10:45). "Whoever believes in the Son has eternal life; whoever does not obey the Son shall not see life, but the wrath of God remains on him" (John 3:36). For any of us, including relativists, who turn from our treason and trust in Jesus, the wrath of God is turned away and eternal life is given.

2) Relativism Cultivates Duplicity

Everyone knows in his heart that believing relativism to be *true* is contradictory, and everyone also knows intuitively that no one even tries to put it into practice consistently. Therefore, both philosophically and practically, it cultivates duplicity. People say they believe in it but do not think or act consistently with what they say. They are hypocrites.

It is contradictory because the very process of thinking about relativism commits you to truths that you do not treat as relative.

Relativists employ the law of noncontradiction and the law of cause and effect whenever they talk about their belief in relativism and its relation to the world. But these laws are not relative.

For example, when they say, "There is no universally valid standard for what is true," they assume several universal standards. One is the law of cause and effect: they believe that in speaking this sentence, a cause is created that will have effects. They do not believe that speaking their mind is pointless. Effects follow from sufficient causes. This is a universal truth that they live by, including the speech that denies it.

Another universal law they assume while denying the existence of universal standards is the law of noncontradiction—namely, that the assertion of a proposition is an implicit denial of its opposite. "Do this" does not mean "don't do this." "God exists" does not mean "God does not exist." The statement "God exists" and "God does not exist" cannot both be true in the same way at the same time. When they say, "There is no universally valid standard for what is true," they assume that this does not mean its opposite. It does not mean: "There *are* universally valid standards for what is true." They assume the law of noncontradiction.

In other words, apart from some universal standards, the relativists could not even formulate the premises and conclusions that they say lead them to relativism. This is a deep duplicity. And when one does it knowingly, it is immoral. The king keeps saying he has clothes on, when he knows he is naked. People keep saying all is relative, when they know their very thinking and talking involves principles that are not relative.

Carnell on the Moral Dimension of Rationality

In 1957 Edward John Carnell published a powerful book called *Christian Commitment: An Apologetic.* Apart from the Scriptures it was probably this book that opened my eyes most to the moral dimension of rationality. In other words, Carnell made clear that there is a profound sense in which being irrational is immoral. He went beyond Descartes' "I think, therefore, I am" and argued, "I think, therefore I am morally obliged to admit the reality of my own existence."[1] Human existence and logical inference are intrinsically moral. He illustrates:

> When Aristotle tried to refute the skeptics, however, he encountered the frustrating fact that the skeptics *used* the law of contradiction to *deny* the law of contradiction. . . . After exhausting all his dialectical powers, Aristotle had to bow to the truth that only men of character can apprehend rational ultimates. . . . Aristotle, like Kant, illuminates the fact that the rational life cannot get on with it unless the moral life is firm.[2]

The Games Professors Play—at School

The immoral dimension of relativism is most obvious when relativists live their lives. They simply do not live them as though relativism were true. Professors may play the academic game of relativism in their classes, but when they go home they get upset when their wives don't understand what they say. Why do they get upset? Because they know that there is an objective meaning that can be transmitted between two human beings, and we have moral obligations to grasp what is meant.

No husband ever said, "Since all truth and language are relative, it does not matter how you interpret my invitation to sleep together." Whether we write love letters, or rental agreements, or instructions to our children, or directions for a friend, or contracts, or sermons, or obituaries, we believe objective meaning exists in what we write, and we expect people to try to understand. And we hold them accountable (and often get upset) if they don't.

Nobody is a relativist when his case is being tried in court and his objective innocence hangs on objective evidence. The whole system of relativism is a morally corrupting impulse. It brings with

---

[1] Edward John Carnell, *Christian Commitment: An Apologetic* (New York: Macmillan, 1957), 37.
[2] Ibid., 39–41.

it duplicity and hypocrisy. It is a great bluff. And what is needed in our day is for many candid children to rise up as in the fairy tale and say, "The king has no clothes on."

3) Relativism Often Conceals Doctrinal Defection

One of the most tragic effects of relativism is the effect it has on language. In a culture where truth is esteemed as something objective and external and valuable, language holds the honorable place of expressing and transmitting that precious cargo of truth. In fact, a person's use of language is assessed on the basis of whether it corresponds to the truth of the reality he expresses.

But when objective truth vanishes in the fog of relativism, the role of language changes dramatically. It's no longer a humble servant for carrying precious truth. Now it throws off the yoke of servanthood and takes on a power of its own. It doesn't submit to objective, external reality; it creates its own reality. It no longer serves to display truth. Now it seeks to obtain the preferences of the speaker.

This gives rise to every manner of spin. The goal of language is no longer the communication of reality but the manipulation of reality. It no longer functions in the glorious capacity of affirming the embrace of truth, but now it functions in the devious capacity of concealing defection from the truth.

Machen on Language as Merely Useful

In 1925 J. Gresham Machen described this relativistic corruption of language in relation to Christian confessional affirmations:

> It makes very little difference how much or how little of the creeds of the Church the Modernist preacher affirms. . . . He might affirm every jot and tittle of the Westminster Confession, for example, and yet be separated by a great gulf from the Reformed Faith. It is not that part is denied and the rest affirmed; but all is denied, because all is affirmed merely as useful or symbolic and not as true.[3]

---

[3]J. Gresham Machen, *What Is Faith?* (1925; repr. Edinburgh: Banner of Truth, 1991), 34.

This utilitarian view of language is the direct fruit of relativism. It leads to evasive, vague speech that enables the relativist to mislead people into thinking he is still orthodox. Here is Machen's amazingly up-to-date description of the mind-set that comes from relativism:

> This temper of mind is hostile to precise definitions. Indeed nothing makes a man more unpopular in the controversies of the present day than an insistence upon definition of terms. . . . Men discourse very eloquently today upon such subjects as God, religion, Christianity, atonement, redemption, faith; but are greatly incensed when they are asked to tell in simple language what they mean by these terms.[4]

In all these ways, relativism corrupts the high calling of language and turns it into a conspirator in covering up the doctrinal defection of those who don't have the courage to publicly renounce historic evangelical faith.

This is the exact opposite of the commitment that Paul had in the way he used language. In 2 Corinthians 4:2 he said, "We have renounced disgraceful, underhanded ways. We refuse to practice cunning or to tamper with God's word, but by the open statement of the truth we would commend ourselves to everyone's conscience in the sight of God." Oh, that every church and school and denomination would write that over every word preached, taught, discussed, and written!

4) Relativism Cloaks Greed with Flattery

Apparently, the apostle Paul was accused in Thessalonica of simply wanting money from his converts. When he responded to this, he showed the link between flattery and greed:

> Our appeal does not spring from error or impurity or any attempt to deceive, but just as we have been approved by God to be entrusted with the gospel, so we speak, not to please man, but to please God who tests

[4]Ibid., 13–14.

our hearts. For we never came with words of *flattery*, as you know, nor with a *pretext for greed*—God is witness. (1 Thess. 2:3–5)

What is flattery? It's the use of language to make someone feel good about himself with a view to getting what you want. Paul calls it a *pretext for greed*. When relativism has abolished truth as the governor of language, language itself goes on sale. If we can get more money by telling people what they want to hear, we will give them what they want.

Relativism is the perfect atmosphere for turning language into a pretext for greed by flattering people with what they want to hear. This is no surprise to Paul. "The time is coming," he says, "when people will not endure sound teaching, but having itching ears they will accumulate for themselves teachers to suit their own passions, and will turn away from listening to the truth" (2 Tim. 4:3–4). Language becomes the lackey of people's passions, not the servant of truth. That is what relativism does.

Against this impulse of relativism, Paul stakes out his position and beckons us to follow: "We are not, like so many, peddlers of God's word, but as men of sincerity, as commissioned by God, in the sight of God we speak in Christ" (2 Cor. 2:17). There is an objective reality called the Word of God. We do not peddle that Word. We speak before the face of God.

5) Relativism Cloaks Pride with the Guise of Humility

On September 9, 1999, the *Minneapolis Star Tribune* carried a lead editorial that said, "Christians must abandon the idea that the Jews must be converted. That idea . . . is one of the greatest scandals in history."[5] So I wrote a letter to the editor and argued that since only he who "has the Son has life" (1 John 5:12), it is not a scandal. Rather, it is love that moves Christians to urge Jewish people to receive Jesus as their Messiah.

---

[5]*Minneapolis Star Tribune*, September 9, 1999, A20.

This letter brought a blistering response from the pastors of four large downtown churches, which said, "Unfortunately 'arrogant' is the right word to describe *any* attempts at proselytizing—in this case the effort of Christians to 'win over' their Jewish brothers and sisters. Thoughtful Christians will disassociate themselves from any such effort."

The point of that story is that if you believe in a truth that all people must embrace in order to be saved, you will be called arrogant. On the other hand, relativism is put forward as the mark of humility. It is not. I don't mean to say that all non-relativists are humble. We are not. We are sinners in need of God's grace. But what I do want to say is that relativism only looks humble but is inherently a cloak of pride.

How Relativism Cloaks Pride

It works like this. Truth with a capital *T*—Truth rooted in God's objective reality and word—is a massive, unchanging reality that we little humans must submit to. Coming to know this truth is the humble task of putting ourselves under this reality and submitting to it. *Understanding* is literally taking the humble position to *stand under* the truth and let it be our rule.

If we do not create reality, but God does, then the more reality we know, the more we must adjust our minds and our lives to that reality. If we try to deny reality, it will have the last word. We may try to reject the objective law of gravity, but if we try to throw off the humble position of submission and jump out a window, our treason will be quickly exposed as folly.

But what about relativism? It poses as humble by saying: "We mere mortals cannot know what the truth is—or even if there *is* any universal truth." This sounds humble. But look carefully at what is happening. It's like a servant saying: "I am not smart enough to know which person here is my master—or if I even have a master." The result is that he doesn't have to submit to any master and can be his own master. His vaunted weakness is a ruse to cover his rebellion against his master.

That is in reality what happens to relativists: in claiming to be too lowly to know the truth, they exalt themselves as supreme arbiters of what they can think and do. This is not humility. This is rooted in deep desire not to be subordinate to the claims of truth. The name for this is *pride*. The only way pride can be conquered in us is for us to believe in Truth and be conquered by it so that it rules us and we don't rule it.[6]

Relativism enables pride to put on humble clothes and parade through the streets. But don't be mistaken. Relativism chooses every turn, every pace, every street, according to its own autonomous preferences, and submits to no truth. We will serve our generation well by exposing the prideful flesh under these humble clothes.[7]

6) Relativism Enslaves People

In John 8:31–32, Jesus said, "If you abide in my word, you are truly my disciples, and you will know the truth, and the truth will set you free." If we cultivate a view of truth that makes it unreachable or nonexistent, then we create a kind of Christianity that will simply colonize slaves. People are not freed from sin and death by the fog of relativism. They stay in chains.

There is a remedy: "Sanctify them in the truth; your word is truth" (John 17:17). But if the people are led away from a love of the truth, they will not be set free, they will not be sanctified, and they will perish. Paul says in 2 Thessalonians 2:10, "[They perish],

---

[6]G. K. Chesterton wrote over a hundred years ago (1908), "What we suffer from today is humility in the wrong place. Modesty has moved from the organ of ambition. Modesty has settled upon the organ of conviction; where it was never meant to be. A man was meant to be doubtful about himself, but undoubting about the truth; this has been exactly reversed. Nowadays the part of a man that a man does assert is exactly the part he ought not to assert—himself. The part he doubts is exactly the part he ought not to doubt—the Divine Reason. . . . We are on the road to producing a race of man too mentally modest to believe in the multiplication table." *Orthodoxy* (Garden City, NY: Doubleday, 1957), 31–32.
[7]For more on the nature of humility, see "Brothers, Don't Confuse Uncertainty with Humility" in John Piper, *Brothers, We Are Not Professionals* (Nashville: Broadman, 2002), 159–66; and "What Is Humility?" available online at http://www.desiringgod.org/ResourceLibrary/TasteAndSee/ByDate/1999/1140.

because they did not receive *the love of the truth* so as to be saved" (NASB). We are not playing games. Relativism leads people away from a love of the truth and so enslaves them and destroys them.

7) Relativism Eventually Leads to Totalitarianism

The formula is simple: when relativism holds sway long enough, everyone begins to do what is right in his own eyes without any regard for submission to truth. In this atmosphere, a society begins to break down. Virtually every structure in a free society depends on a measure of integrity—that is, submission to the truth. When the chaos of relativism reaches a certain point, the people will welcome any ruler who can bring some semblance of order and security. So a dictator steps forward and crushes the chaos with absolute control. Ironically, relativism—the great lover of unfettered freedom—destroys freedom in the end. Michael Novak put it powerfully like this:

> Totalitarianism, as Mussolini defined it, is . . . the will to power, unchecked by any regard for truth. To surrender the claims of truth upon humans is to surrender Earth to thugs. It is to make a mockery of those who endured agonies for truth and the hands of torturers.
>
> Vulgar relativism is an invisible gas, odorless, deadly, that is now polluting every free society on earth. It is a gas that attacks the central nervous system of moral striving. The most perilous threat to the free society today is, therefore, neither political nor economic. It is the poisonous, corrupting culture of relativism. . . .
>
> During the next hundred years, the question for those who love liberty is whether we can survive the most insidious and duplicitous attacks from within, from those who undermine the virtues of our people, doing in advance the work of the Father of Lies. "There is no such thing as truth," they teach even the little ones. "Truth is bondage. Believe what seems right to you. There are as many truths as there are individuals. Follow your feelings. Do as you please. Get in touch with your self. Do what feels comfortable." Those who speak in this way prepare the jails of the twenty-first century. They do the work of tyrants.[8]

---

[8]Michael Novak, "Awakening from Nihilism: The Templeton Prize Address," *First Things* 45 (August/September, 1994): 20–21.

The Bondage of Relativism

The list of damaging effects of relativism could go on. I have not spoken of the multicultural relativism that silences the prophetic indictment of the destructive forces of personal and social dysfunction. I have not spoken of the poisonous effects of relativism on personal integrity as it erodes the sacred duty to tell the truth and keep one's word. But perhaps this is enough.

Remember the chief priests and the elders in Matthew 21:23–27 from the previous chapter? Because they had no intention of submitting to the truth, they were trapped. If we say John's baptism is "from heaven," we will be shamed for not believing. So we can't say that is true. If we say it's "from man," we will be mobbed, because they say he's a prophet. So we can't say that is true. So we will make up a truth. We will say, "We don't know." What bondage! They cannot own the truth because they are enslaved to the fear of shame and harm.

And what a prostitution of the gift of thinking! How seriously they thought! How carefully. Their minds were in full force. "If we say this . . . then that." "But if we say that . . . then this." "Ah, conclusion: we don't know." They thought they had escaped. They thought this was freedom.

This is what happens to reason and language—thinking and speaking—when the roots of relativism are spreading. This is not what thinking is for. It is God's gift. Together with gospel-liberation, and prayer, and the illumining work of the Holy Spirit, the gift of thinking can know the truth and be free indeed.

The chief priests and the elders were enslaved to the fear of being shamed and being hurt. Or to put it another way: they were in bondage to the craving for the praise of man and the pleasures of security. Either way, what governed the use of their minds was this fear and this craving.

The Gospel Frees Us to See and Speak the Truth

Jesus came into the world and died for our sins to set us free from this slavery. When God is for us in Christ (Rom. 8:31), we do not need the praise of man. When God promises to be with us (Heb. 13:5) and work all things for our good (Rom. 8:28), the power of fear is broken. This is why the gospel makes us rational—not rationalistic, but simply free to see and speak the truth.[9]

When you are deeply peaceful and confident that, because of Christ, God will bring you safely to his eternal kingdom and be the all-satisfying Treasure of your life forever, then you are free to see the truth, and love the truth, and speak the truth no matter what, and joyfully spread a passion for the truth whose name is Jesus.

---

[9]What I mean by *rationalistic* is suggested by the way G. K. Chesterton warns us: "The madman is not the man who has lost his reason. The madman is the man who has lost everything except his reason." "The poet only asks to get his head into the heavens. It is the logician who seeks to get the heavens into his head. And it is his head that splits." In other words, the poet is "rational" the way I am using the term—he is humble enough to freely delight in what heaven really has to reveal. *Orthodoxy*, 17–19.

Facing the
Challenge of
Anti-intellectualism

I do not undervalue education, but really I have seen so many of these educated preachers who forcibly reminded me of lettuce growing under the shade of a peach tree, or like a gosling that had got the straddles by wading in the dew, that I turn away sick and faint. . . .

Peter Cartwright

9

Unhelpful Anti-intellectual Impulses in Our History

Evangelist Billy Sunday, who died in 1935, spoke for many Christians when he said, "If I had a million dollars I'd give $999,999 to the church and $1 to education."[1] This might not be a bad idea if the church took responsibility for education. But that's not what he meant. This is the voice of thousands who are deeply suspicious of any emphasis on thinking in the pursuit of God—like the emphasis of this book.

American Partners: Pragmatism and Subjectivism

The America that produced Billy Sunday was an America on its way to the triumph of pragmatism and subjectivism. Not that Sunday was unprincipled, but his hostility to the life of the mind diminished the ability of the church to stand against destructive uses of the mind—like pragmatism and subjectivism.

These two views have triumphed for many people in our culture—and in our churches.[2] *Subjectivism* says that thinking is useful

---

[1]Quoted in Richard Hofstadter, *Anti-Intellectualism in American Life* (New York: Vintage, 1962), 122.
[2]One of the best books documenting this is David Wells, *No Place for Truth, Or: Whatever Happened to Evangelical Theology?* (Grand Rapids: Eerdmans, 1993). "Many of those whose task it is to broker the truth of God to the people of God in the churches have now redefined the pastoral task such that theology has become an embarrassing encumbrance or a matter of which they have little knowl-

as a means of justifying subjective desires. *Pragmatism* says that thinking is useful as a means of making things work. To be sure, these forces can produce striking achievements in science and business and industry. But missing from both views is the conviction that thinking is a gift of God, whose chief role is to pursue and love and live by ultimate truth.

Pragmatism and subjectivism obscure the reality of truth. They engage the mind, but they make it the servant of our desires and our work. But they can't answer which desires I should pursue and which work is worthwhile. On this point Nicholas Wolterstorff, who taught philosophy at Calvin College for thirty years and at Yale University for fifteen years, wrote in his relevant review of Richard Sennett's book *The Craftsman* that Sennett argues that a craftsman is one who is dedicated to doing good work for its own sake. "The craftsman's 'primordial mark of identity' is that he or she is focused on achieving quality, on doing good work. Craftsmanship is quality-driven work."[3] Then Wolterstorff makes this probing observation:

> There is something deficient about the person who does good work for its own sake without ever asking whether it's a good thing that this work be done. The estimable craftsman asks two questions concerning the good. He asks whether what he is doing or making for its own sake is a good example of its kind: a good violin, a good arpeggio, and so forth. But he also asks whether doing or making a good example of this kind is a good thing to do.[4]

Wolterstorff illustrates the need for these larger questions by referring to Robert Oppenheimer, who is often known as "the father

---

edge. . . . I look at the way in which the pastorate has become professionalized, how the central function of the pastor has changed from that of truth broker to manager of the small enterprises we call churches. To the extent that this tendency has taken root, I have concluded that it is producing a new generation of pastoral disablers" (pp. 6, 13). "As the nostrums of the therapeutic age supplant confession, and as preaching is psychologized, the meaning of Christian faith becomes privatized. At a single stroke, confession is eviscerated and reflection reduced mainly to thought about one's self. . . . Thus it is that the pastor seeks to embody what modernity admires and to redefine what pastoral ministry now means in light of this culture's two most admired types, the manager and the psychologist" (p. 101).
[3] Nicholas Wolterstorff, "Thinking with Your Hands," in *Books and Culture* 15 (March/April 2009): 30.
[4] Ibid.

of the Atomic bomb." "Oppenheimer came to know what a good bomb is and obsessively devoted himself to trying to make one; what he did *not* do at the time is ask himself whether making this good bomb was a good thing to do."[5]

That kind of question touches on truth that transcends individual preference. Answers to such questions come from a way of thinking that is very different from subjectivism and pragmatism. Ultimately, it has to come finally from the knowledge of God. And the point of this book is that thinking is essential in knowing God.

A Tradition of Underwhelming Support for Thinking

But there is a long history of Christians going the other direction. They have seen the powerful use of the mind in the pursuit of empty things—whole industries of education and entertainment that ignore God and promote things contrary to his will. They have seen the brilliant scientific horrors of the modern world as well as the blessings—two world wars and multiple holocausts in Germany and Asia and Africa, as well as electricity and refrigeration and underground sewer systems and antibiotics.

The fruit of thinking is ambiguous in the secular world. And in the church a long line of faithful servants of Christ, like Billy Sunday, have decided that the life of the mind has done more harm than good. America, in particular, has a long history of evangelical suspicion of education and intellectual labor. Before Billy Sunday, evangelist Charles Finney lamented that ministers were coming "out of college with hearts as hard as the college walls."[6]

Peter Cartwright, the untiring Methodist leader, wrote in his autobiography in 1856:

> The illiterate Methodist preachers actually set the world on fire (the American world at least) while they were lighting their matches! . . . I do not undervalue education, but really I have seen so many of these

---

[5]Ibid.
[6]Quoted in Hofstadter, *Anti-Intellectualism*, 94.

educated preachers who forcibly reminded me of lettuce growing under the shade of a peach tree, or like a gosling that had got the straddles by wading in the dew, that I turn away sick and faint. . . . What has a learned ministry done for the world, that have studied divinity as a science?[7]

Similarly D. L. Moody debunked formal theology. When asked about his own, he said, "My theology! I didn't know I had any. I wish you would tell me what my theology is."[8]

Behind this negative attitude toward intellectual effort lay very genuine and legitimate concerns. The concerns came from certain perceived antagonisms. Whether we believe these are real or fictional will shape much of our intellectual life. Richard Hofstadter expresses the antagonisms as follows:

Intellect is pitted against feeling, on the ground that it is somehow inconsistent with warm emotion. It is pitted against character, because it is widely believed that intellect stands for mere cleverness, which transmutes easily into the sly or the diabolical. It is pitted against practicality, since the theory is held to be opposed to practice, and the "purely" theoretical mind is so much disesteemed. It is pitted against democracy, since intellect is felt to be a form of distinction that defies egalitarianism.[9]

These perceived antagonisms are still very much alive today. Who has not heard a very learned discourse and felt that the speaker was out of touch with real life, especially at the relational and emotional level? There really does seem to be something about the life of the mind that is inhospitable to other kinds of human experience that we cherish, and that may be even more important.

Not Thinking Is No Solution for Thinking Arrogantly

My response to these indictments of intellectual effort is not that they are wrong, but that the solution is not to abandon rigorous thinking.

---

[7] Quoted in ibid., 102–3.
[8] Quoted in ibid., 108.
[9] Ibid., 45–46.

If we were to succeed in raising a generation of people who give up serious, faithful, coherent thinking, we will have raised a generation incapable of reading the Bible. I argued in chapter 1 that reading *is* thinking. Either we do it carefully and accurately or we do it carelessly and inaccurately. The problem with those who debunk the gift of thinking as a way of knowing God is that they do not spell out clearly what the alternative is. The reason is that there isn't one. If we abandon thinking, we abandon the Bible, and if we abandon the Bible we abandon God.

The Holy Spirit has not promised a shortcut to the knowledge of God. He inspired the prophets and apostles to write in a book what he showed them and told them. In more than one place, he even said explicitly that reading the book is the God-appointed way of knowing mysteries of God. For example, in Ephesians 3:3–4 Paul wrote that "the mystery was made known to me by revelation." The question is: How will that wonderful knowledge of God's mystery be made known to the rest of us? He answers in verse 4: "When you read this, you can perceive my insight into the mystery of Christ."

The word *when* is not there in the original Greek. There is a simple participle: "Reading [*anaginōskontes*] you are able to consider [or think about, *noēsai*] my insight into the mystery of Christ." The most natural meaning of this participle is this: "*By means of* reading . . . " Reading is the way we are able to think the thoughts of Paul and thus know the mystery of God.

It is therefore futile counsel to tell the church that thinking is worthless. There is no reading without thinking. And there is no reading carefully and faithfully and coherently without thinking carefully and faithfully and coherently. The remedy for barren intellectualism is not anti-intellectualism, but humble, faithful, prayerful, Spirit-dependent, rigorous thinking.

Ripley's Resistance and the Appeal to Scripture

Consider one more voice from history lifted against the dangers of leaning on logic and learning. This voice is significant here because it moves from the more familiar complaints to more substantive ones. These more substantive ones appeal to the passages of the Scriptures themselves that seem to rise up against the human mind.

In the 1830s a Unitarian pastor named George Ripley became disillusioned with Unitarianism. His conversion was not to evangelical Christianity but to a new movement called transcendentalism. He was driven by his opposition to the intellectualism of his alma mater, Harvard Divinity School.

Instead of embracing biblical doctrine, he embraced intuition as a source of spiritual transcendence. Ironically this move inclined him to criticize Harvard in a way that expressed what many evangelicals thought about the intellectual life. It is a classic statement of the anti-intellectual sentiments that mark this history of America and the evangelical movement that shaped so much of it. In 1839 he wrote:

> I have known great and beneficial effects to arise from the simple exhibition of the truth of the Gospel to the heart and conscience, by earnest men, who trusted in the intuitive power of the soul, for the perception of its divinity. . . .
>
> Much as I value a sound logic in its proper place, I am sure it is not the instrument which is mighty through God to the pulling down of the strongholds of sin. It may detect error; but it cannot give so much as a glimpse of the glory of Christ. It may refute fallacies; but it cannot bind the heart to the love of holiness. . . . You maintain, that "extensive learning" is usually requisite for those who would influence their fellow man on religious subjects.
>
> But Jesus certainly did not take this into consideration in the selection of the twelve from the mass of the disciples; he committed the promulgation of his religion to "unlearned and ignorant" men; the sublimest truths were entrusted to the most common minds; and, in this way, "God made foolish the wisdom of the world." . . . Christ . . . saw that the parade of wisdom, which books impart, was as nothing before "the light that enlighteneth every human mind."
>
> The whole course of this nation's history was an illustration of the fact "that mechanics are wont to be God's great ambassadors to mankind." . . . Christ established no college of apostles; he did not revive the

school of the prophets which had died out; he paid no distinguished respect to the pride of learning; indeed, he sometimes intimates that it is an obstacle to the perception of truth; and thanks God [sic] that, while he has hid the mysteries of the kingdom of heaven from the wise and prudent, he has made them known to men as ignorant as babes of the lore of the schools.[10]

There are six assertions here that call into question the rigorous use of the mind in knowing God and helping others know him. I will give brief responses to the first four and then deal more thoroughly with the last two in the next two chapters.

The Weakness of Logic in the Battle with Sin

Ripley's first assertion is that (1) *sound logic is not the instrument "which is mighty through God to the pulling down of the strongholds of sin."*

This is a reference to 2 Corinthians 10:4–5: "The weapons of our warfare are not of the flesh but have divine power to destroy strongholds. We destroy arguments and every lofty opinion raised against the knowledge of God, and take every thought captive to obey Christ." Ripley concludes: logic is not "mighty through God to the pulling down of the strongholds of sin."

This is true if by "logic" he means "logic alone." The goal of bringing ourselves or others to a true and sin-conquering knowledge of God will never be reached by the instrument of logic alone. Jesus sent Paul on an impossible mission. He said to Paul, "I am sending you to open their eyes, so that they may turn from darkness to light and from the power of Satan to God, that they may receive forgiveness of sins" (Acts 26:17–18). This is what happens when strongholds are destroyed, and arguments against the truth of God are overcome, and thoughts are taken captive for Christ.

This is supernatural work. The eyes of the mind and heart do not open automatically. Logic alone cannot bring it about. That's why

---

[10]Quoted in ibid., 48 n. 8.

Paul said, "No one can say 'Jesus is Lord' *except in the Holy Spirit*" (1 Cor. 12:3). No logical argument for the lordship of Christ will bring about submission, apart from the work of the Holy Spirit. This is also why Jesus responded to Peter's recognition of him with the words, "Flesh and blood has not revealed this to you, but my Father who is in heaven" (Matt. 16:17).

Paul knew this. Nevertheless, what a powerful use he made of his mind in the battle for human souls! Here's his custom illustrated in the way he tried to open eyes in Thessalonica:

> Paul went in, *as was his custom*, and on three Sabbath days *he reasoned* with them from the Scriptures, explaining and proving that it was necessary for the Christ to suffer and to rise from the dead, and saying, "This Jesus, whom I proclaim to you, is the Christ." And some of them were persuaded and joined Paul and Silas, as did a great many of the devout Greeks and not a few of the leading women. (Acts 17:2–4)

Even though logic will not open the eyes of the spiritually blind, using human reason to present Christ clearly and with some rational force was the approach that the apostle Paul took. The effect in Thessalonica was that "some of them were persuaded." God broke through and opened their eyes (see also Acts 19:8–9).

So the answer to Mr. Ripley is that a logical presentation of the gospel of Christ is like wire along which the electricity of spiritual power runs. Wires do not make lights go on; electricity does. But in the providence of God, electricity runs through wires. And in the design of God, the use of our minds in knowing, ordering, and presenting the truth of Christ is the normal way that the eyes of the blind are opened and belief in Jesus is awakened.

"Sanctify Them in the Truth"

This is our answer to Ripley's next two assertions as well. He says, (2) *logic may "detect error; but it cannot give so much as a glimpse of the glory of Christ"* (2 Cor. 4:4). And he says, (3) *logic "may refute fallacies;*

but it cannot bind the heart to the love of holiness." Again this is true if he means "logic alone."

But we have seen in our treatment of 2 Corinthians 4:4–6 (in chapter 3) that glimpsing the glory of Christ is the effect of two things, not just one thing. It is the effect of God's supernatural work of shining light into our hearts (v. 6); and it is the effect of Paul's proclaiming Jesus as Lord (v. 5). This proclamation—even if it is the simplest of gospel messages—involves logic and reasoning. There is no glimpsing of Christ without the "electricity" of supernatural illumination. And there is no glimpsing without the human wire of thoughtful proclamation.

And the same is true of sanctification. When Ripley says that logic "may refute fallacies; but it cannot bind the heart to the love of holiness," he leads people away from a very serious truth. Jesus said, "Sanctify them in the truth; your word is truth" (John 17:17); and, "You will know the truth, and the truth will set you free" (John 8:32). Knowing the truth with our minds and holding fast to it as a treasure in our hearts is the key to holiness.

Over and over the New Testament says that our "knowing" truth leads to holy behavior. "Your boasting is not good. *Do you not know* that a little leaven leavens the whole lump?" (1 Cor. 5:6). "*Do you not know* that your bodies are members of Christ? Shall I then take the members of Christ and make them members of a prostitute?" (1 Cor. 6:15). "*Do you not know* that friendship with the world is enmity with God? *Therefore* whoever wishes to be a friend of the world makes himself an enemy of God" (James 4:4). The fact that some people "know" these things and still sin means only that there is more to it than knowing, but not less.

I Am Pleading for Fiery Thinking, Not Formal Education

Ripley's fourth assertion helps me clarify the aim of this book. He says that (4) *Christ did not see "extensive learning" as essential, but "committed the promulgation of his religion to 'unlearned and ignorant' men"* (see Acts 4:13). I totally agree that "extensive learning" is not essential to the spread of the gospel or the deep knowledge of God. This book is not written to defend "extensive learning."

There is no necessary correlation between extensive learning and the right use of the mind. Many PhDs think poorly, and many people with little formal education think with great clarity and depth. I am pleading for a hearty engagement of the mind in the pursuit of God. I am not pleading mainly for more formal education. That may or may not be good in different cases. But the right use of the mind is always good no matter how much or how little education one has.

Is the Bible a Witness for the Prosecution?

Ripley's final two assertions are the most serious. He refers to passages of Scripture that warn against the dangers of "the wisdom of the world," and he points out the darkened condition of the "wise and prudent" (KJV). (5) His fifth assertion is simply a quotation of 1 Corinthians 1:20: *"Has not God made foolish the wisdom of the world?"* (6) And his sixth assertion is a quotation of Luke 10:21: *"You have hidden these things from the wise and understanding and revealed them to little children."* To these we turn in the next two chapters.

[Jesus] rejoiced in the Holy Spirit and said,
"I thank you, Father, Lord of heaven and earth,
that you have hidden these things from the wise
and understanding and revealed them to little children;
yes, Father, for such was your gracious will.
All things have been handed over to me by my Father,
and no one knows who the Son is except the Father,
or who the Father is except the Son and anyone to whom
the Son chooses to reveal him." Then turning to the disciples
he said privately, "Blessed are the eyes that see what you see!
For I tell you that many prophets and kings desired
to see what you see, and did not see it,
and to hear what you hear, and did not hear it."

Luke 10:17–24

10

You Have Hidden These Things from the Wise and Understanding

In the previous chapter we began to look at George Ripley's reasons for being so suspicious of the human intellect. He expressed these reasons almost two hundred years ago, but two of them are of unusual importance because they deal with the very words of Jesus and the great apostle Paul.[1] He refers to two passages of Scripture. He is asking, in essence, If thinking is so important in coming to know God, why would Jesus say, "I thank you, Father, Lord of heaven and earth, that you have hidden these things from the wise and understanding and revealed them to little children" (Luke 10:21)? And why does the apostle Paul say, "Has not God made foolish the wisdom of the world?" (1 Cor. 1:20)?

These two passages become the two pillars of his anti-intellectualism. So I am going to take them seriously and try to show that they are very shaky pillars for supporting the house of anti-intellectualism. In this chapter, we will begin to deal with Luke 10:21. Then in chapter 11, we will consider 1 Corinthians 1:20 and come back to Luke 10:21 at the end of chapter 11 to show how the two passages are amazingly similar in what they teach.

---

[1] Richard Hofstadter, *Anti-Intellectualism in American Life* (New York: Vintage, 1962), 48 n. 16.

A Rare and Remarkable Place for Jesus to Rejoice

Here's the context for the first concern from Luke 10:21:

> The seventy-two returned with joy, saying, "Lord, even the demons are subject to us in your name!" And he said to them, "I saw Satan fall like lightning from heaven. Behold, I have given you authority to tread on serpents and scorpions, and over all the power of the enemy, and nothing shall hurt you. Nevertheless, do not rejoice in this, that the spirits are subject to you, but rejoice that your names are written in heaven." In that same hour he rejoiced in the Holy Spirit and said, "I thank you, Father, Lord of heaven and earth, that you have hidden these things from the wise and understanding and revealed them to little children; yes, Father, for such was your gracious will. All things have been handed over to me by my Father, and no one knows who the Son is except the Father, or who the Father is except the Son and anyone to whom the Son chooses to reveal him." Then turning to the disciples he said privately, "Blessed are the eyes that see what you see! For I tell you that many prophets and kings desired to see what you see, and did not see it, and to hear what you hear, and did not hear it." (Luke 10:17–24)

There are only two places in the Gospels where Jesus is portrayed as actually rejoicing.[2] One is John 11:14–15: "Then Jesus told [his disciples] plainly, 'Lazarus has died, and for your sake *I am glad* that I was not there, so that you may believe.'" Jesus prioritizes faith so far above this life that he rejoiced that he was not there to save Lazarus's life so that the faith of his disciples would be strengthened. That is one instance of Jesus' rejoicing.

The other is found here in Luke 10:21. Luke tells us that Jesus' joy focuses on the hiding of something from "the wise and understanding" and the revealing of something to "little children." "He rejoiced . . . and said, 'I thank you, Father . . . that you have hidden . . . and have revealed.'" To understand why Jesus rejoiced in

---

[2]There are other references to Christ's joy (John 15:11; 17:13) but not to an instance of his present act of rejoicing. His earthly pilgrimage was a season of great burden-bearing. "He was despised and rejected by men; a *man of sorrows*, and acquainted with grief" (Isa. 53:3). In view of Paul's expression, "sorrowful, yet always rejoicing" (2 Cor. 6:10), we do not have to think that Jesus was ever without the perfect measure of joy for his situation.

this hiding and revealing, and to see its wider implications for the Christian task of thinking, we need to clarify what was being hidden, what was being revealed, and to whom each was happening.

What Is God Happy to Hide?

What was it that the Father had hidden from some and revealed to others? From the wider context we would say with I. Howard Marshall that it included "the gospel of the kingdom, attested by the preaching and mighty works of Jesus."[3] We say this because the specific occasion for Jesus' joy was the return of the seventy whom he had sent out to preach, "The kingdom of God has come near to you" (Luke 10:9, 11). Therefore we can see that what was being hidden and revealed was the presence of the kingdom of God in the ministry of Jesus.

This is confirmed in verses 23–24 where Jesus says, "Blessed are the eyes that see what you see! For I tell you that many prophets and kings desired to see what you see, and did not see it, and to hear what you hear, and did not hear it." The reason their eyes are "blessed" is that these are the ones to whom the Father has revealed what he has hidden from others. Jesus is saying that what has been revealed to these "little children" is what prophets and kings in the Old Testament longed to see and did not see. The most natural understanding of what was revealed is the appearing of the Messiah to establish the kingdom of God. That is what prophets longed to see.

Jesus himself is the Messiah, and he is now, in a way they did not expect, inaugurating his kingdom. It is not with armies and political power. It is by his own obedience and suffering and death and resurrection. The mystery of the kingdom is that the fulfillment of the Messiah's kingdom happens in history long before its glorious, global consummation.[4]

We can see these two stages of fulfillment—the already and the

---

[3] I. Howard Marshall, *Commentary on Luke* (Grand Rapids: Eerdmans, 1978), 434.

[4] "The mystery of the Kingdom is the coming of the Kingdom into history in advance of its apocalyptic manifestation. It is, in short, 'fulfillment without consummation.'" George Ladd, *The Presence of the Future* (Grand Rapids: Eerdmans, 1974), 222.

not yet of the kingdom of God—in Luke 17:24–25: "As the lightning flashes and lights up the sky from one side to the other, so will the Son of Man be in his day. But first he must suffer many things and be rejected by this generation." There is a first coming of the Messiah to suffer and a second coming in glorious triumph. This was so unexpected for most Jewish people, who expected only one glorious coming, that it was very hard to grasp. This is what was being hidden from some and revealed to others. But this is not the heart of what is being revealed.

Heart of the Matter: Who Are the Father and the Son?

The heart of the matter is more personal. The closer context to Luke 10:21 tells us more specifically what is being hidden and what is being revealed. Immediately after Jesus said that he rejoiced over the Father's hiding and revealing work, he said in Luke 10:22, "All things have been handed over to me by my Father, and no one knows who the Son is except the Father, or who the Father is except the Son and anyone to whom the Son chooses to reveal him." Notice the word *reveal*. In verse 21 Jesus said he was glad that the Father has "*revealed* [these things] to little children," and in verse 22 Jesus says that he and the Father alone know something that others can know only if it is *revealed* to them.

So the "revealing" in verse 22 is surely the same as the "revealing" in verse 21. What is this revelation? It is the true identity of the Father and the Son. "No one knows who the Son is except the Father, and who the Father is except the Son." This is what is hidden from some and revealed to others in verse 21.

Is It the Son or the Father Who Is Revealing and Concealing?

But notice something strange here. In verse 21 Jesus says that it is God the Father who is hiding and revealing: "Father, . . . you have hidden these things from the wise and understanding and revealed them to little children." But in verse 22 Jesus says that he himself, the Son, is doing the revealing: "No one knows who . . . the Father is except the Son and anyone *to whom the Son chooses to reveal him.*"

So how do these two revealings relate to each other—what the Father does and what the Son does? As we have seen from the wider context, the revealing that the Father does (Luke 10:21) is the truth about the mystery of the kingdom of the Messiah—that the kingdom has come in Jesus and that he is truly the Messiah and that the time is fulfilled (Luke 10:23–24). This fits with the statement of verse 22 that "no one knows who the Son is except the Father." The recognition of Jesus as the Messiah and the Son of God is the work of God the Father in the minds and hearts of the "little children."

Peter's Way of Knowing

This is exactly confirmed in Matthew 16:15–17 where Jesus asked the disciples, "Who do you say that I am?" Peter answered, "You are the Christ [the Messiah], the Son of the living God." To which Jesus responded, "Blessed are you, Simon Bar-Jonah! For flesh and blood has not revealed this to you, but my Father who is in heaven." This shows that what the Father revealed to some and not to others is the true identity of Jesus; he is the Messiah, the Son of the living God. "Flesh and blood" (that is, what we are by mere human nature[5]) cannot recognize the messiahship or the deity of Jesus for what it really is. God the Father must reveal this to us.

On the other hand, it is plain from Luke 10:22 that what the Son reveals is the true identity of the Father. "No one knows . . . who the Father is except the Son and anyone to whom the Son chooses to reveal him." So how then do these two acts of revelation relate to each other—the Father's revelation of the Son, and the Son's revelation of the Father?

---

[5]The evidence for this is found in 1 Cor. 15:50; Gal. 1:16; Eph. 6:12; Heb. 2:14.

In one sense there is a sequence from stage one of the Father's work in revealing the Son to stage two of the Son's work in revealing the Father. In another sense, these revelations are simultaneous.

Stage One in Knowing the Father: Coming to the Son

In the first sense, to know the Father, one must come to the Son. When Philip said to Jesus, "Lord, show us the Father," Jesus said to him, "Have I been with you so long, and you still do not know me, Philip? Whoever has seen me has seen the Father" (John 14:8–9). So knowing the Father happens in coming to the Son. Thus the work of the Father in revealing the Son appears to precede the work of the Son in revealing the Father.

This is surely implied in John 6:44 where Jesus says, "No one can come to me unless the Father who sent me draws him." In other words, before the Son can reveal the Father to someone, that person has to come to the Son. But coming to the Son is owing to the Son-revealing work of the Father in doing what he did for Peter to draw him to the Son: "Flesh and blood did not reveal [my true identity] to you [Peter], but my Father who is in heaven." In revealing the truth about Jesus to Peter, the Father drew him to Jesus.

Stage Two in Knowing the Father: Ongoing Fellowship with Jesus

Now, in fellowship with Jesus, we come to know the true identity of the Father. This is the second stage in the sequence: "No one knows . . . who the Father is except the Son and anyone to whom the Son chooses to reveal him" (Luke 10:22). First, we come to Jesus because the Father has revealed to us that he is "the Christ, the Son of the living God." Second, Jesus reveals to us God the Father in his ever-increasing fullness.

This is the sequence Jesus describes in John 17:6 when he prays to his Father, "I have manifested your name to the people whom you gave me out of the world. Yours they were, and you gave them to me, and they have kept your word." The Father draws people to the Son—that is, gives them to the Son—and then the Son manifests the Father to them.

Does the Father or the Son Choose to Reveal the Father?

But there are two problems with saying it like that. One is that this appears to contradict Luke 10:22, which stresses that *the Son* is the one who chooses those to whom he will reveal the Father. "No one knows . . . who the Father is except the Son and anyone to whom *the Son chooses* to reveal him." The choice of the Son is emphasized in this verse. He chooses the ones to whom he reveals the Father. But it appears from what we have said so far that *the Father* is making that decisive choice in "giving" people to the Son (John 17:6) and "drawing" people to the Son (John 6:44).

The other problem with the way we have said it so far is that describing it as a two-step sequence, beginning with the Father's revealing the Son followed by the Son's revealing the Father, obscures a deeper unity in these two acts. These two acts of revealing are, in fact, simultaneous. They are distinct, but not separate.

When the Father reveals the Son's true identity, he reveals him as the true Revelation *of God the Father*. "Whoever has seen me has seen the Father" (John 14:9). Therefore, in one sense, to see the *Son* for who he really is, is simultaneously to see the *Father* in him. That's what it means to see Jesus for who he really is—God incarnate, Immanuel, God with us, "the glory of God in the face of Jesus Christ" (as Paul said in 2 Cor. 4:6).

It is not wrong to say there is sequence, because we do go on seeing more and more of God the Father as we abide in Christ and continue our fellowship with him. But it is profoundly important to see that recognizing Jesus for who he really is (the image of God the Father) involves a simultaneous recognition of who the Father really is (the One revealed in Jesus Christ).

Seeing this helps us solve the other problem I mentioned, namely, that the Father's choosing who will see the Son seems to preempt the Son's choosing who will see the Father (Luke 10:22). What we have now seen is that the Father's work in revealing the Son and the Son's work in revealing the Father are so united that they are inseparable and simultaneous.

Whatever the Father Does, the Son Does

This is what Jesus seems to say in John 5:19: "Truly, truly, I say to you, the Son can do nothing of his own accord, but only what he sees the Father doing. For whatever the Father does, that the Son does likewise." In other words, the Father and the Son are so profoundly united that it is no contradiction to say, on the one hand, that Jesus chooses the ones to whom he will reveal the Father, and, on the other hand, that Jesus reveals the Father to those whom the Father chooses to give him.

When Jesus says in Luke 10:22, "All things have been handed over to me by my Father," he does not mean that the Father ceased to have what he handed over to the Son. Rather it means that the Son would now, in this world, have the authority of the Father to call and reveal and save and judge. Therefore, even though Jesus said, "No one can come to me unless the Father who sent me draws him," (John 6:44), he also said, "I have other sheep that are not of this fold. I must bring them also" (John 10:16). The Father must draw them. And the Son must bring them. These are not separate acts. "I and the Father are one" (John 10:30). The Son is in the Father's choosing to reveal, and the Father is in the Son's choosing to reveal. Father and Son conspire to reveal the fullness of each other's true identity and glory.

My Answer

That is my answer to the question, "What is being hidden and revealed in Luke 10:21?" What is being hidden and revealed is not just the presence of the kingdom but the true personal identity and divine glory of the messianic King and his Father.

Keep in mind that we are trying to answer why it is that Jesus rejoices in hiding and revealing this truth. "[Jesus] *rejoiced* in the Holy Spirit and said, 'I thank you, Father, Lord of heaven and earth, that you have hidden these things from the wise and understanding and revealed them to little children'" (Luke 10:21). Now we can see more clearly that the joy of Jesus in this hiding and revealing is also the joy of God the Father. They are one in this act of concealing and revealing.

The New Question: From Whom Is This Concealed?

So our question now becomes, "*From whom* are these things being hidden, and *to whom* are they being revealed?" If we know this, we may be able to answer why the Father and the Son rejoiced in this hiding and revealing.

Jesus says that these things are hidden from "the wise and understanding," but to the "little children" they are revealed. It is plain from verse 23 that the term "little children" does not refer to six-month-old babies. The reference in that verse is to the disciples. "Turning to *the disciples* [Jesus] said privately, 'Blessed are the eyes that see the things you see!'" So the disciples are among the "little children" that get the "blessing" of seeing what the Son chooses to reveal.

So "the wise and understanding" and "little children" are two kinds of persons beyond infancy. They are not literal infants. But what kind of persons are they?

Not All the Wise Are Rejected

Not all "wise ones" are viewed in a negative light. For example, Jesus said, "Therefore I send you prophets and *wise men* and scribes, some of whom you will kill and crucify, and some you will flog in your synagogues and persecute from town to town" (Matt. 23:34). Here "wise ones" (same word as in Luke 10:21) are the true emissaries of Jesus—his apostles or missionaries. These "wise ones" are not confounded. They have received the message of Jesus and are speaking in his name. So it will not do to say that *all* wisdom is contrary to the revelation of God. Jesus must have in view different kinds of wisdom and different kinds of "wise ones."

Not All Childlikeness Is Good

Not only that, but being "little children" is not always viewed as praiseworthy. For example, Paul warned against the weakness and vulnerability of a child's mental condition when he said that pastors and teachers equip the saints "so that we may *no longer be children, tossed to and fro by the waves and carried about by every wind of doctrine, by human cunning, by craftiness in deceitful schemes*" (Eph. 4:14).

Instead we are to be mature and thoughtful and discerning, using our minds to spot and avoid crafty winds of false doctrine. "Brothers, *do not be children* in your thinking. Be infants in evil, but in your thinking be mature" (1 Cor. 14:20). So it is plain that not everything about infants or children is worthy of imitation, especially not their gullibility.

The Humility of Childlikeness Is Key

On the other hand, Jesus was fond of putting children forward as the kind of people who would "receive the kingdom." "Truly, I say to you, whoever does not receive the kingdom of God like a child shall not enter it" (Mark 10:15). "Let the little children come to me and do not hinder them, for to such belongs the kingdom of heaven" (Matt. 19:14). "Truly, I say to you, unless you turn and become like children, you will never enter the kingdom of heaven. Whoever humbles himself like this child is the greatest in the kingdom of heaven" (Matt. 18:3–4).

It appears from this last text (Matt. 18:4) that the aspect of childlikeness that Jesus affirms is humility. "Whoever *humbles* himself like this child . . . " He probably does not mean that children are by nature humble, but they are, as children, *pictures* of humility. That is, they are happy to depend on their parents for help in all their obvious helplessness. The smallest ones can't feed themselves. They can't clean themselves. They can't move about on their own. They can't clothe or protect themselves. They are utterly dependent on someone to care for them and to meet their needs. Jesus is speaking of a kind of person who is deeply dependent and humble enough to receive the help he really needs from God.

Presumably, then, the "wise and understanding" are proud. Is this the key to why truth is hidden from them but revealed to "little children"? Is this the key to Jesus' joy in such hiding and revealing? Before completing the answer, I have found it very illuminating to turn to the place where the apostle Paul dealt with this very issue—wisdom hidden from the wise. So we now turn to Paul, and then at the end of chapter 11 we will return to Luke 10:21.

Where is the one who is wise? Where is the scribe?
Where is the debater of this age?
Has not God made foolish the wisdom of the world?
For since, in the wisdom of God, the world did not know God
through wisdom, it pleased God through the folly of
what we preach to save those who believe.
For Jews demand signs and Greeks seek wisdom,
but we preach Christ crucified, a stumbling block to Jews
and folly to Gentiles, but to those who are called,
both Jews and Greeks, Christ the power of God
and the wisdom of God.

1 Corinthians 1:20-24

11

In the Wisdom of God, the World Did Not Know God through Wisdom

We are still testing two increasingly shaky pillars of anti-intellectualism. One is the statement of Jesus that God has "hidden [his truth] from the wise and understanding and revealed [it] to little children" (Luke 10:21). We began in the previous chapter to wrestle with this because it seems, on the surface, to undermine the main point of this book, namely, that thinking is essential in coming to know God; and mature thinking is needed in order to know God maturely. Jesus seems to exalt children and put down the intelligent. We will come back to this at the end of the chapter.

Listening to Jesus' Apostle Deal with Our Issue

But before completing the treatment of Luke 10:21, it will be helpful to watch the apostle Paul wrestle with this very same issue. So let's listen first to Paul's treatment in 1 Corinthians 1:17–2:16, which is the one passage in all the Bible that deals most extensively with this very issue of "the wise and understanding" in relation to God's "hidden" wisdom.

In 1 Corinthians 1:19 Paul quotes Isaiah 29:14 and says, "It is written, 'I will destroy the wisdom of the wise, and the discernment of the discerning I will thwart.'" In the original Greek, the words behind "the wise" and "the discerning" are exactly the same as the words behind "the wise" and "the understanding" in Luke 10:21 ("I thank you, Father, Lord of heaven and earth, that you have hidden these things from the wise and understanding and revealed them to little children"). So it seems, from the similarity in terminology, that we are dealing with the same issue in the early chapters of 1 Corinthians as Jesus was dealing with in Luke 10:21–22, namely, a certain kind of "wisdom and understanding" that alienates a person from God and his truth.

Divine Wisdom Decreed That Human Wisdom Would Not Find Him

Paul also speaks of the wisdom of God being hidden, as Jesus did in Luke 10:21. For example, in 1 Corinthians 1:21 Paul says that "*in the wisdom of God* the world by its wisdom did not know God" (NET). In other words, God decided *in his wisdom* that human wisdom would not be the path to knowing God. God's wisdom dictated that he should hide himself from "[the world's] wisdom."

Again, in 1 Corinthians 2:7–8 Paul says, "We impart a secret and hidden wisdom of God, which God decreed before the ages for our glory. None of the rulers of this age understood this, for if they had, they would not have crucified the Lord of glory." God's wisdom is not a wisdom of this age, and so the "rulers of this age" were blind to it. It was concealed from them. God's plan was, as Jesus said, to hide his wisdom (including his true identity) from most of the "wise and understanding."

Similarly, Paul says in 1 Corinthians 1:26–27, "Consider your calling, brothers: not many of you were wise according to worldly standards. . . . But God chose what is foolish in the world to shame the wise." God chose to do this. That's what Jesus said too in Luke 10:21. He chose to pass over most of "the wise" when he did his "calling" and revealing work. So it is clear that Paul is dealing with a divinely revealed wisdom that is hidden from some and revealed to others, similar to the way Jesus spoke of it in Luke 10:21.

Two Kinds of Wisdom and Two Kinds of Wise Persons

The idea of "wisdom" for Paul was loaded with negative and positive freight in 1 Corinthians. Positively, he says:

- The preaching of Christ crucified is "the wisdom of God" (1:24).
- Christ himself "became to us wisdom from God" (1:30).
- "Yet among the mature we do impart wisdom" (2:6).
- "We impart a secret and hidden wisdom of God, which God decreed before the ages for our glory" (2:7).

So there is, in Paul's way of thinking, a "wisdom" that is entirely positive. On the other hand, there is a wisdom Paul regards as negative:

- "Christ did not send me to baptize but to preach the gospel, and *not with words of eloquent wisdom*" (1:17).
- "Where is the one who is wise? . . . Has not God made foolish the wisdom of the world?" (1:20).
- "Greeks seek wisdom, but we preach Christ crucified" (1:22–23).
- "The foolishness of God is wiser than men" (1:25).
- "Consider your calling, brothers: not many of you were wise according to worldly standards" (1:26).
- "I . . . did not come proclaiming to you the testimony of God with lofty speech or wisdom" (2:1).
- "My speech and my message were not in plausible words of wisdom, but in demonstration of the Spirit and of power" (2:4).
- ". . . that your faith might not rest in the wisdom of men but in the power of God" (2:5).
- "We impart this in words not taught by human wisdom but taught by the Spirit" (2:13).
- "If anyone among you thinks that he is wise in this age, let him become a fool that he may become wise. For the wisdom of this world is folly with God. For it is written, 'He catches the wise in their craftiness,' and again, 'The Lord knows the thoughts of the wise, that they are futile'" (3:18–20).

All these uses of the word "wisdom" are negative.

God's Wisdom versus Man's Wisdom

What is the difference between the wisdom that Paul denounces and the wisdom that he loves? We can see the ultimate answer to this question in the terms that describe the two kinds of wisdom. One kind is described as the "wisdom of the world" (1:20; 3:19), the "wisdom of men" (2:5), the wisdom "according to worldly standards" (1:26), and "human wisdom" (2:13). The other kind of wisdom is described three times as the "wisdom of God" (1:24; 2:7) and once as "not a wisdom of this age" (2:6). So the ultimate difference between these two kinds of wisdom is that one is God's and one is man's.

What then is the difference between man's wisdom and God's wisdom? One way to answer this question is to notice from 1 Corinthians 1:17 and 23 that human wisdom nullifies the meaning of the cross of Christ, but God's wisdom upholds the meaning of the cross. Paul says that if he had come preaching "in wisdom of word" (literal translation), the cross of Christ would "be emptied of its power" (1:17). And he adds that "the Greeks seek [human] wisdom" and therefore regard the preaching of the cross as "folly" (1:23). So there is something about "human wisdom" that nullifies the cross by regarding it as foolishness, when, in fact, the cross is "the wisdom of God" (1:24).

The Cross Is the Continental Divide between Human Wisdom and Divine Wisdom

We may say then that a fundamental difference between divine wisdom and human wisdom is that God's wisdom exalts what the cross stands for and human wisdom is offended by what the cross stands for. What does it stand for? The cross stands for the ungodliness and helplessness of man (Rom. 5:6), the undeserved grace of God (Rom. 3:24), and the unimpeachable justice of God (Rom. 3:25–26).

In other words, what offends human wisdom about the cross is that it humbles man and exalts the unearnable grace of God. It makes humans look dependent and helpless—like little children—and makes God look all-sufficient and all-providing and absolutely free in giving salvation to sinners.

The reason the cross is called "the wisdom of God" (1 Cor. 1:24) is that the heart of God's wisdom is his commitment, in the work of salvation, to uphold and exalt the glory of God's grace for the ever-lasting enjoyment of his people. You can see God's glory and our joy come together in 1 Corinthians 2:9. Paul describes the content of God's wisdom as "what God has prepared for those who love him." And what is that? Ephesians 2:7 answers: God saved us "so that in the coming ages he might show the immeasurable riches of his grace in kindness toward us in Christ Jesus."

So the heart of God's wisdom is God's passion to display the glory of his grace in Christ for the everlasting enjoyment of those who believe. Since we are all undeserving sinners, the cross is central to this wisdom. Without the cross we could not have this wisdom.

Wisdom Comes in a Way that Confounds Boasting

Thus the nature of God's wisdom governs the way it is revealed and known, namely, in a way that will subdue our boasting in ourselves and sustain our boasting in the Lord. We can see this most explicitly in 1 Corinthians 1:27–30 where Paul says that "God chose what is foolish in the world . . . so that no human being might boast in the presence of God."

We see it also in 1 Corinthians 3:20–21: "'The Lord knows the thoughts of the wise, that they are futile.' So let no one boast in men. For all things are yours." Since God's wisdom aims to exalt the glory of God's grace in Christ crucified, God reveals this wisdom in a way that nullifies human pride and boasting.

To put it positively, Paul adds in 1 Corinthians 1:30–31 that Christ crucified "became to us wisdom from God . . . as it is written,

'Let the one who boasts, boast in the Lord.'" In other words, the wisdom of God designs not only that we *not* boast in ourselves but that we *do* boast in Christ. The essence of God's wisdom is to exalt the glory of his grace manifest in Christ crucified.

God Opposes Humans' Finding Him through Their Own Wisdom

We can see the essence of divine wisdom in one of the most remarkable verses in this section, and one that is most like Luke 10:21, where Jesus rejoices that God has "hidden these things from the wise and understanding." In 1 Corinthians 1:21 Paul says that "in the wisdom of God, the world did not know God through wisdom." Notice the words "in the wisdom of God." This means that God's wisdom designed that humans would not know God through their wisdom.

After all that we have seen about the nature and goal of God's wisdom, we can now see the reason for this. If humans found God and knew God by their native wisdom and intelligence, they would be able to boast that they had penetrated the distance between God and man. They would have overcome the distance not only between finiteness and infinity but also between sin and holiness. To prevent this kind of boasting, God did not design the world this way. "*In the wisdom of God*, the world did not know God through wisdom." God planned this kind of hiding.

In the wisdom of God, "it pleased God through the folly of what we preach to save those who believe" (1 Cor. 1:21). This so-called "folly of what we preach" is the word of the cross—foolishness in man's eyes, but wisdom in God's eyes. So knowing God through the wisdom of the world is contrasted with being saved by believing the message about Christ crucified.

The point here is that there is no true knowledge of God and no salvation apart from childlike dependence on the grace of God in Christ crucified. If we are not willing to see ourselves as helpless, ungodly sinners and cast ourselves for mercy on the grace of God in Christ, we will not know God or be saved by him.

The Ultimate Difference between God's Wisdom and Man's Wisdom

Therefore, we may conclude that the ultimate difference between God's wisdom and man's wisdom is how they relate to the glory of God's grace in Christ crucified. *God's wisdom* makes the glory of God's grace our supreme treasure. But *man's wisdom* delights in seeing himself as resourceful, self-sufficient, self-determining, and not utterly dependent on God's free grace.

Divine wisdom begins consciously with God ("The fear of the LORD is the beginning of wisdom," Ps. 111:10), and is consciously sustained by God and has the glory of God as its conscious goal. Divine wisdom reached its climactic demonstration in the cross of Christ—because the cross was a way of salvation that humbles man and exalts the grace of God. When divine wisdom is revealed to humans in the death of Christ, its effect is to save us and humble us by doing for us what we could not do for ourselves.

Back to the Last Chapter's Questions

Now we are in a position to answer more surely the questions raised in the previous chapter from Luke 10:21. There Luke tells us that Jesus "rejoiced in the Holy Spirit and said, 'I thank you, Father, Lord of heaven and earth, that you have hidden these things from the wise and understanding and revealed them to little children.'" Who are these "wise and understanding" and these "little children"? What we have seen in Paul fits with what we saw in Luke.

The Little Children

The "little children" are those who know and feel themselves helpless and unworthy of any good from God. They have renounced all pride and boasting. They do not feel resourceful in themselves to know God or to save themselves from judgment. They admit that without special, divine revelation they will not know the most important reality and will not know how to live according to the truth. They humbly admit that if they ever know God for who he really is, it will be owing to the same wonderful work of divine grace that Jesus spoke over Peter's confession: "Flesh and blood has not revealed this to you, but my Father who is in heaven" (Matt. 16:17).

The "little children" on this side of the cross know that they are utterly dependent on the death of Christ to save them and to open the door to wisdom. Without his atoning, substitutionary death, all access to God and his wisdom would be cut off. The "little children" admit with longing and hope and confidence that Christ is the way to wisdom, and the sum of all wisdom (1 Cor. 1:30; Col. 2:3).

These "little children" are the "spiritual" ones that Paul refers to in 1 Corinthians 2:15—the ones whom the Spirit of God has humbled so that they can see the death of Christ as the glorious wisdom of God. To such ones the Father reveals the Son, and the Son reveals the Father. They are the ones who receive the word of the cross because it is not foolishness to them. By grace their child-likeness is located in the right place: "Brothers, do not be children in your thinking. Be infants in evil, but in your thinking be mature" (1 Cor. 14:20).

The Wise and Understanding

"The wise and understanding," on the other hand, are offended by the "word of the cross." To them it is foolishness because the cross makes clear the helplessness and unworthiness of all human beings. The cross exalts God's grace and undermines all boasting except in the Lord. But self-exaltation and self-determination are the deep pleasures of "the wise and understanding." Therefore they are resistant to anything that contradicts their sense of self-sufficiency and resourcefulness. They want to take credit for and be praised for their intellectual accomplishments.

The wisdom of "the wise and understanding" has produced remarkable scientific advances. But it leaves out the most important reality, namely, God. From one side it is stunning for its achievements, and from another side it is stunning for its stupidity in missing the main thing. The wisdom of "the wise and understanding" does not begin with God; it is not conscious of being sustained by God, and it rejects God's purpose for the universe, which is to display the glory of God chiefly through Christ crucified for sinners.

The "wise and understanding" exult in "the wisdom of the world," which is deeply committed to making man (or creation) the measure of all things rather than God the Creator. This wisdom stands in the service of human pride and upholds it with its distinguished accomplishments. These are the people from whom God hides himself, according to Luke 10:21 and 1 Corinthians 1:21.

God Rejoices to Hide from the Humanly Wise

Not only does God hide himself, but Luke 10:21 says he rejoices to do this. "[Jesus] rejoiced in the Holy Spirit and said, 'I thank you, Father, Lord of heaven and earth, that you have hidden these things from the wise and understanding and revealed them to little children; yes, Father, for such was your gracious will" (or, literally, "such was well pleasing to you," *eudokia*).

Paul makes the same point in 1 Corinthians 1:21 with a word closely related to the word for "well pleasing" in Luke 10:21: "For since, in the wisdom of God, the world did not know God through wisdom, it *pleased* [*eudokēsen*] God through the folly of what we preach to save those who believe." God delights in what his own wisdom dictates. He finds it "well pleasing." So when God's wisdom dictates that pride-preserving human wisdom will not come to know God, and instead childlike dependence on Christ comes to know God, he delights in this. It is well pleasing to him.

Whence Then This Divine Pleasure?

Now we are in a position to answer the question, Why does God (Father, Son, and Holy Spirit[1]) rejoice in hiding himself from "the wise and understanding" and revealing himself to "little children"? To see the answer most fully, we need to realize that God's joy is ultimately in the display of his own glory—especially the glory of his grace.[2] In Isaiah 2:17, the prophet says, "The haughtiness of man shall be humbled, and the lofty pride of men shall be brought low, and the LORD alone will be exalted in that day." God's goal in the history of redemption is to humble the suicidal pride of man and exalt the glory of his grace in the Christ-exalting worship of his people. Therefore, he takes pleasure in everything that contributes to this.

Therefore, God delights in revealing himself to "little children" because this highlights God's all-sufficiency rather than man's. The "little children" despair of self-sufficiency and look away from their helplessness and sinfulness to the grace of God in Christ. Therefore the motive of God to reveal himself to such ones is that it displays more clearly the beauty and worth of his grace. The heart of these "little children" magnifies the grace of God, while the heart of "the wise and understanding" magnifies man's self-determination and self-sufficiency. Therefore God's joy in displaying the glory of his grace is the reason he rejoices in revealing that glory to "little children."

On the other hand, he hides it from "the wise and understanding" because if they came to know God without becoming "little

---

[1] That the Holy Spirit is included in this pleasure is plain from Luke 10:21 when Luke says that "[Jesus] rejoiced in the Holy Spirit." I take that to mean that his joy in the Father's acts of hiding and revealing was prompted and thus approved by the Spirit.

[2] I have argued for this in great detail in *The Pleasures of God: Meditations on God's Delight in Being God*, 2nd ed. (Sisters, OR: Multnomah, 2000), 97–120; and *Let the Nations Be Glad: The Supremacy of God in Missions*, third edition (Grand Rapids: Baker, 2010), 39–46.

children," the glory of God's grace and the power of the cross of Christ would be obscured. It would not be plain that the "wise ones" were utterly dependent on God for their wisdom and their salvation. They would boast that by their own wisdom and resourcefulness they found God. To such ones Jesus says, "Unless you turn and become like children, you will never enter the kingdom of heaven" (Matt. 18:3).

The Hiddenness of God and the Happiness of His People

God's wisdom in designing things this way not only brings *him* joy but also leads to the greatest joy of *his people*. Their greatest joy is joy in God. This is plain from Psalm 16:11: "You [God] make known to me the path of life; in your presence there is fullness of joy; at your right hand are pleasures forevermore." *Fullness* of joy and *eternal* joy cannot be improved. Nothing is fuller than full, and nothing is longer than eternal. And this joy is owing to the presence of God, not the accomplishments of man.

Therefore, in order to love us infinitely and delight us fully and eternally, God, through the cross of Christ, secures for us the one thing that will satisfy us totally and eternally, namely, the vindication and experience of the infinite worth of his own glory. He alone is the source of full and lasting pleasure. Therefore, his commitment to uphold and display his glory is not the mark of a megalomaniac but the mark of love.

If he revealed himself to the proud and self-sufficient and not to the humble and dependent, he would obscure the very glory whose worth is the focus of our joy. Therefore, God hides himself from "the wise and understanding" and reveals himself to "little children," because he rejoices in the glory of his grace and the greatness of our joy.

Either or Neither May Be Educated

What we have seen now in chapters 10 and 11 is that the terms "wise and understanding" and "little children" in Luke 10:21 do not correspond simply to "educated" and "uneducated." Jesus is not saying that the uneducated get the grace of revelation and the educated don't. To put it another way, there are "little children" among the educated and there are boastful among the uneducated. Norval Geldenhuys is right when he comments on Luke 10:21 with these words:

> The contrast pointed [out] by the Savior is not that between "educated" and "uneducated" but between those who imagine themselves to be wise and sensible and want to test the Gospel truths by their own intellects and to pronounce judgment according to their self-formed ideas and those who live under the profound impression that by their own insight and their own reasonings they are utterly powerless to understand the truths of God and to accept them. Often "unlearned" persons are in the highest degree self-opinionated as regards spiritual matters, and on the other hand some of the most learned are humble and childlike and accept the truths of the Gospel unreservedly. Jesus makes the contrast not between educated and uneducated but between people with the wrong and self-sufficient attitude and those with the right and childlike attitude.[3]

Therefore, the warnings that Jesus and Paul have sounded in Luke 10:21 and 1 Corinthians 1:21 are not warnings against careful, faithful, rigorous, coherent thinking in the pursuit of God. In fact, the way Jesus and Paul spoke these very warnings compels us to engage in serious thinking even to understand them. And what we find is that pride is no respecter of persons—the serious thinkers may be humble. And the careless mystics may be arrogant.

The aim of this book is to encourage serious, faithful, humble thinking that leads to the true knowledge of God, which leads to loving him, which overflows in loving others. There is such a way of thinking, from the simplest insights of the common man to the highest halls of learning. In the next chapter, we will catch a glimpse of it in Paul's amazing warning against the knowledge that puffs up.

---

[3]Norval Geldenhuys, *The Gospel of Luke* (Grand Rapids: Eerdmans, 1977), 306–7.

Finding a
Humble Way
of Knowing

Now concerning food offered to idols:
we know that "all of us possess knowledge."
This "knowledge" puffs up, but love builds up.
If anyone imagines that he knows something,
he does not yet know as he ought to know.
But if anyone loves God, he is known by God. Therefore,
as to the eating of food offered to idols, we know that
"an idol has no real existence," and that "there is no God but one." . . .
However, not all possess this knowledge. . . . Take care
that this right of yours does not somehow become a
stumbling block to the weak. For if anyone sees you who have
knowledge eating in an idol's temple, will he not be encouraged,
if his conscience is weak, to eat food offered to idols?
And so by your knowledge this weak person is destroyed,
the brother for whom Christ died.

1 Corinthians 8:1–11

12

The Knowledge That Loves

In the previous three chapters, we have pressed on the pillars of anti-intellectualism and found them too shaky to trust. They do not hold up to biblical analysis. They have an appearance of stability because pride is ever lurking at the door of the mind. But that is true for both the educated and the uneducated. We tend to feel proud of knowledge we have that others don't have. For the educated, this knowledge may come from much work and superior IQ. For the uneducated, it may come from private revelations, or mystical experiences, or the school of hard knocks that the pampered professors don't experience. But the solution to arrogant thinking—educated and uneducated—is not no thinking. It is the right kind of thinking. That is what this chapter is about.

Blunt and Almost Baffling

Our starting point is Paul's blunt and puzzling statement in 1 Corinthians 8:1–3. It forges a link with the theme of the previous chapter—loving God with your mind.

> Now concerning food offered to idols: we know that "all of us possess knowledge." This "knowledge" puffs up, but love builds up. If anyone

> imagines that he knows something, he does not yet know as he ought
> to know. But if anyone loves God, he is known by God.

The sequence of thought here is almost baffling. Gordon Fee says, "The most striking thing about this opening paragraph is how non sequitur it seems to be."[1] Yes, "seems" is the right word. Paul would take us deeper by making us think.

Smart, Proud, and Loveless

At this point in 1 Corinthians, Paul is taking up the issue of whether Christians can eat food offered to idols. After these introductory sentences, he continues, "Therefore, as to the eating of food offered to idols, we *know* that 'an idol has no real existence,' and that 'there is no God but one'" (1 Cor. 8:4). Notice the word *know*. This "knowledge" (which is true) had become a cause for being "puffed up" for some at Corinth. How do we know this? Because verses 7, 9, and 11 show that some in the church were using this knowledge to flaunt their right to eat freely without any care for the weaker Christians.

Paul warns them that "not all possess this knowledge" (v. 7)—contrary to what they were saying ("all of us possess knowledge"). That means those who do not have that knowledge are liable to drawing destructive conclusions from others' freedom to eat all things. So he pleads with them to act lovingly: "Take care that this right of yours does not somehow become a stumbling block to the weak" (v. 9). He cautioned them not to handle their "knowledge" so carelessly, because "by your knowledge this weak person is destroyed" (v. 11).

So the issue in Corinth is that knowledge was producing pride, and pride was destroying love. So he says, "This 'knowledge' puffs up, but love builds up." Knowledge is susceptible to pride because it is the result of getting, not giving. Knowledge is a possession. It is something we have attained. So we are prone to boast about it.

---

[1]Gordon H. Fee, *The First Epistle to the Corinthians* (Grand Rapids: Eerdmans, 1987), 364.

Love, on the other hand, is the act of giving, not getting. Love is not an attainment or an acquisition. It moves outward. It shares. It takes thought for the interest of others. It builds up the faith of others rather than the ego of the lover.

You Don't Know as You Ought to Know

Now, how does Paul go on to speak of this knowledge that is puffing them up? He says in verse 2, "If anyone imagines that he knows something, he does not yet know as he ought to know." This does not mean that Paul thinks Christians can't know things. Ten times in this letter he upbraids the Corinthians for not knowing crucial things about God and life that they should have known (3:16; 5:6; 6:2–3, 9, 15–16, 19; 9:13, 24).

When Paul criticizes them for "thinking that they know something," he has their attitude in mind. They "know" in one sense. But they don't know "as they ought to know." And therefore, in a profound sense, they don't know at all. They don't have the only kind of knowledge that will count in the end. They *imagine* that they know.

This is profound. Paul is saying that knowing (and the thinking that produced it) is not true knowing just because it contains right doctrine about food offered to idols. They knew some true facts about God and about their freedom, but Paul said that they only *imagined* that they know. In other words, this was not true knowledge. They did not know as they ought to know, and so they did not know truly. They imagined that they knew.

True Knowing Loves People

So the crucial question is: "What would turn this imagined knowing into true knowing?" In other words, what does it mean to know as one ought to know? To think as one ought to think? The answer is in the text *before* and *behind*.

Before, Paul had said love builds up (v. 1). That implies that any knowledge that does not stand in the service of love is not real knowing. It is prostituted knowing. It's as though God put surgical tools in our hands and taught us how to save the sick, but we turned them into a clever juggling act while the patients died. Knowing and thinking exist for the sake of love—for the sake of building people up in faith. Thinking that produces pride instead of love is not true thinking. We only imagine that we are thinking. God does not see it as thinking. It's not surgery; it's juggling.

True Knowing Loves God

In seeking to understand what verse 2 means by saying we do "not yet know as [we] ought to know," I said that the answer is in the text *before* and *behind*. We just saw it before in verse 1: "Love builds up."

Now *behind* (in v. 3): "But if anyone loves God, he is known by God." Paul virtually equates knowing as we ought to know with loving God. In connection with verse 1, he makes loving *people* the criterion of true knowing. And in connection with verse 3, he makes loving *God* the criterion of true knowing.

Now we see the link between this text and the point of chapter 6 on loving God with all our mind. That's what the mind is for. And here Paul is saying that loving God is what you are doing when you "know as [you] ought to know." In his view, thinking and knowing are given to us by God for the purpose of loving God and loving people.

Being Known Is Beneath Knowing

But in verse 3 Paul does not simply relate loving God to knowing as we ought to know. He says, "But if anyone loves God, he is known by God." What is the point of saying, "He is known by God"? This is parallel to Galatians 4:9: "But now that you have come to know God, or rather *to be known by God*, how can you turn back again to the weak and worthless elementary principles of the world?" Deeper than knowing God is being known by God. What defines us as Christians is not most profoundly that we have come to know him but that he took note of us and made us his own.

Being known by God is another way of talking about election—God's freely choosing us for himself, in spite of our not deserving it. It's the kind of knowing referred to in Amos 3:2: "You only have I *known* of all the families of the earth." God had chosen Israel as his people, though they were no better than any others.

What Paul is doing when he says, "If anyone loves God, he is known by God," is reminding the proud Corinthians that loving God, not loveless knowledge, is the sign of being among the elect.[2] He is reminding them that everything they have is owing to God's free and sovereign initiative. It's the same as what he had said earlier: "What do you have that you did not receive? If then you received it, why do you boast as if you did not receive it?" (1 Cor. 4:7). The point of 1 Corinthians 8:3 is that "if a man loves God, this is a sign that God has taken the initiative."[3]

Two Remedies for Pride

Paul made that point because pride was the problem. The Corinthians were "puffed up" with their "knowledge." Paul's first remedy for that disease was to say that true knowing and true thinking produce not pride but love for God and love for people. His deeper remedy for the disease of pride was to say that even our love is owing to something prior to our initiative. It is due to God's free gift—God's election.[4] If we love God, and thus know as we ought to know, it is because we have been known—chosen—by God.

Neglecting Knowledge Is Not the Path to Love

I conclude from all this that it is just as dangerous to neglect knowledge as it is to make knowledge a ground of boasting. If there is a

---

[2]"Love . . . is therefore the true sign of election." J. Héring, *The First Epistle of St. Paul to the Corinthians* (Eng. trans., London: Epworth Press, 1962), 68.

[3]C. K. Barrett, *The First Epistle to the Corinthians* (New York: Harper & Row, 1968), 190.

[4]"The only perfect knowledge, both loving and practical, is given by God. . . . To be known by God means to belong to him . . . chosen by God." Quoted from Pere C. Spicq, "Agape in the New Testament," in Anthony Thistleton, *The First Epistle to the Corinthians* (Grand Rapids: Eerdmans, 2000), 627.

way to "know as we ought to know," and if the aim of that knowing is loving God and man, then to neglect that knowing will undermine love. We are not safe from pride if we neglect serious thinking and turn away from knowledge. "My people are destroyed for lack of knowledge" (Hos. 4:6). "My people go into exile for lack of knowledge" (Isa. 5:13).

Zealous for God, but Not Saved

Some people think that zeal for God is all that is needed. But the Bible is shockingly clear that we can have a zeal for God and not be saved. In Romans 10:1 Paul says, "My heart's desire and prayer to God for [my Jewish kinsmen] is that they may be saved." Why aren't they saved? The next verse answers: because "they have a zeal for God . . . " Pause. Let that sink in. "I am praying for them to be saved, because they have a zeal for God . . . "

This is astonishing. You can have a zeal for God and not be saved. The reason this is so astonishing is that the New Testament also says that you cannot be saved without a zeal for God—at least not without the seeds of it. Jesus said to the church in Laodicea, "Because you are lukewarm, and neither hot nor cold, I will spit you out of my mouth" (Rev. 3:16). And Paul says in 1 Corinthians 16:22, "If anyone has no love for the Lord, let him be accursed."

Zeal Needs to Know How God Saves

So we must have a zeal for God, yet if we have it we may not be saved. Why? Paul tells us plainly: "Brothers, my heart's desire and prayer to God for them is that they may be saved. For I bear them witness that they have a zeal for God, *but not according to knowledge*" (Rom. 10:1–2). There's the problem. There is a zeal for God that *accords with knowledge*, and there is a zeal for God that is *not* in accord with knowledge. The one is essential; the other is suicidal. The reason Paul's kinsmen are not saved is that they have a zeal for God that is not in accord with knowledge.

This means that there is a knowledge that turns perishing zeal into saving zeal. What is that knowledge? Romans 10:3 tells us what they didn't know: "They have a zeal for God, but not according to knowledge. For, *being ignorant of the righteousness of God*, and seeking to establish their own, they did not submit to God's righteousness" (Rom. 10:2–3).

Here is the root of their suicidal zeal for God. In all their thinking about God and his righteousness, they missed the main point—that it is a free gift for faith. When they seek to *establish their own* righteousness, they are not *submitting* to the righteousness of God. In fact, their effort to establish their own righteousness is rebellion and insubordination against the righteousness of God. This is why they are not saved.

What's Wrong with Trying to Be Righteous?

But you can hear the zealous kinsmen of Paul cry out in defense: "Wait a minute! You do us entirely wrong. It is precisely our effort to establish righteousness in our lives that *is* our submission to God's righteousness. What else would subjection to God's righteousness look like, except the zeal to establish righteousness in our lives so that it comes into conformity to God's righteousness? What would you want us to do—be indifferent to whether we are righteous or not?"

But Paul says that when you live this way—when you labor to show yourself righteous so that God will accept you—you are *not* submitting to God's righteousness; you are in rebellion against God. Why? Because God's righteousness is a gift of free and sovereign grace, not a merited attainment by human effort—or even a Spirit-wrought performance of relative success in godliness (sanctification). And since it is always and entirely a free gift, submission to it means receiving righteousness as a gift.

The way that gift comes is described in Romans 10:4: "For Christ is the end of the law for righteousness to everyone who believes."

All of God's law was leading to Christ for righteousness for all who believe. By faith we receive Christ. And in Christ we have the righteousness of God. "For our sake he made him to be sin who knew no sin, so that *in him we might become the righteousness of God*" (2 Cor. 5:21). This is what they were ignorant of, and therefore, Paul says, they had a zeal for God and were not saved.

Ignorance That Does Not Excuse

What kind of ignorance was this? It was the same kind of ignorance that we saw in 1 Corinthians 8:2: "If anyone imagines that he knows something, he does not yet know as he ought to know." They knew so much. They knew the law better than we do. But they did not know as they ought to know. Why not? The root was the same for the Corinthians and for Paul's kinsmen—pride. The knowledge they had was puffing them up. It was not humbling them and making them look away from themselves.

So both groups had knowledge. Both groups used their minds to increase knowledge. And both groups were puffed up. What they needed was not less knowledge. The solution to their problem was not to stop thinking. The solution was the heartfelt discovery of God's grace in Jesus Christ. The Corinthians needed to see that everything they knew was a free gift of electing grace and was designed by God to feed the fires of humble love for God and man. Similarly Paul's kinsmen needed to see that the righteousness of God that they lacked was a free gift of that same grace. It comes only through union with Christ by faith. And when it comes, it brings in its train the power to love (Rom. 13:8; Gal. 5:6).

Thinking: The Humble Task of Cutting Wood for the Fire

The lesson from 1 Corinthians 8:1–3 and Romans 10:1–4 is that thinking is dangerous and indispensable. Without a profound work of grace in the heart, knowledge—the fruit of thinking—puffs up. But with that grace, thinking opens the door of humble knowledge. And that knowledge is the fuel of the fire of love for God and man. If we turn away from serious thinking in our pursuit of God, that fire will eventually go out.

He has delivered us from the domain of darkness
and transferred us to the kingdom of his beloved Son,
in whom we have redemption, the forgiveness of sins.
He is the image of the invisible God, the firstborn of all creation.
For by him all things were created, in heaven and on earth,
visible and invisible, whether thrones or dominions
or rulers or authorities—all things were created
through him and for him.

Colossians 1:13–16

From him and through him and to him are all things.
To him be glory forever. Amen.

Romans 11:36

13

All Scholarship Is for the Love of God and Man

The implication of what we saw in chapter 12 is that all thinking—all learning, all education, all schooling, formal or informal, simple or sophisticated—exists for the love of God and the love of man. It exists to help us know God more so that we may treasure him more. It exists to bring as much good to other people as we can—especially the eternal good of enjoying God through Christ.

In this chapter we take the truth of 1 Corinthians 8:1–3 and apply it not to the knowledge of God through Scripture but to the knowledge of God through his other "book," the created world of nature and human life.

Intellectual Insurrection

We love God more fully when we see his glory more fully. That glory is revealed supremely in Jesus Christ and the history of redemption recorded in the Bible. But his glory is also revealed in all that he has made (Ps. 19:1; Rom. 1:19–21). And that revelation through nature includes the revelation of Jesus Christ, because "all things were made through him, and without him was not any thing made that was made" (John 1:3). That was spoken of the Son of God, who in the fullness of time "became flesh and dwelt among us" (John 1:14).

The apostle Paul worshiped Christ for the same reason: "All things were created through him and for him" (Col. 1:16). All the natural world was created through and for Jesus. This is a spectacular statement. Every scholar who devotes himself to observing the world should think long and hard about the words "All things were created . . . *for Christ*." Surely, the least we can say is that this means all thinking—all scholarship—of every kind exists ultimately to discover and display the glory of God, that is, the glory of Jesus Christ, in his Word and in his world. Let every reference to God in the rest of this chapter be heard as a reference to all the persons of the Trinity.

Therefore, the task of all Christian scholarship—not just biblical studies—is to study reality as a manifestation of God's glory, to speak and write about it with accuracy, and to savor the beauty of God in it, and to make it serve the good of man. It is an abdication of scholarship when Christians do academic work with little reference to God. If all the universe and everything in it exists by the design of an infinite, personal God, to make his manifold glory known and loved, then to treat any subject without reference to God's glory is not scholarship but insurrection.

Not Knowing Things for What They Are

Christian scholarship is not threatened but served when it is permeated by spiritual affections for the glory of God in all things. Most scholars know that without the support of observable objects to deal with (texts, witnesses, chemicals, people, behavior, etc.), affections degenerate into groundless emotionalism. But not as many scholars recognize the converse: that without the awakening of true spiritual affections, seeing the fullness of truth in all things is impossible. Without a spiritual wakefulness to divine purposes and connections in all things, we will not know things for what they truly are.

One might object that the subject matter of psychology or sociology or anthropology or history or physics or chemistry or English or computer science is not about "divine connections and purposes" but simply about natural connections. But that would miss the point: to see reality in the fullness of truth, we must see it in relation to God, who created it, and sustains it, and gives it all its properties, relations, and designs. Therefore, we cannot do Christian scholarship if we have no spiritual sense or taste for God—no capacity to apprehend his glory in the things he has made.

To See, You Must Have Eyes

Jonathan Edwards showed from Scripture that this "spiritual sense" is given by God through supernatural new birth, effected by the word of God: "The first effect of the power of God in the heart in regeneration, is to give the heart a divine taste or sense; to cause it to have a relish of the loveliness and sweetness of the supreme excellency of the divine nature."[1] Therefore, to do Christian scholarship, a person must be born again. That is, a person must not only *see* the effects of God's work in the world but also *savor* the beauty of God's nature in the gospel, and in all that he has made, and in all that he does.

But it is not in vain to do rational work with rigorous observation; it is essential. This is true, even though everything hangs on God's free gift of spiritual life and sight. The reason, as Edwards says, is that "the more you have of a rational knowledge of divine things, the more opportunity will there be, when the Spirit shall be breathed into your heart, to see the excellency of these things, and to taste the sweetness of them."[2]

Even though Edwards said this mainly about the "rational knowledge" of *Scripture* and theology, it applies, in a lesser degree, to *all knowledge* gained by exacting observation and by careful thought

---

[1]Jonathan Edwards, "Treatise on Grace," in *Treatise on Grace and Other Posthumously Published Writings*, ed. Paul Helm (Cambridge, UK: James Clarke, 1971), 49. For a fuller treatment of this understanding of the new birth, see John Piper, *Finally Alive: What Happens When We Are Born Again* (Fearn Ross-Shire, UK: Christian Focus, 2009).

[2]"Christian Knowledge," in *The Works of Jonathan Edwards*, vol. 2 (Edinburgh: Banner of Truth, 1974), 162.

about God's created world. God exhibits his glory in the created reality that is studied by the scholar (Ps. 19:1; 104:31; Rom. 1:19–21; Col. 1:16–17). Therefore, the severe disciplines of seeing what is there, and analyzing its parts, and studying its relations are essential for Christian scholarship.

God's goal in the exhibition of his glory through the created world is not realized if the scholar does not see and savor that glory. On the contrary, the magnifying of God's glory is in and through the seeing and savoring of the scholar's mind and heart. When the excellence of God's glory echoes in the affections of God's scholar and resounds through his creating and speaking and writing, God's aim for Christian scholarship is advanced.

The Pervasive Obstacle of Pride

It is plain, then, that one great obstacle to great Christian scholarship is pride. The humility of wisdom is the happy consciousness that all things come from God, are sustained by God, and exist for God. This wisdom is rooted in the pride-destroying, joy-giving cross of Christ. Such scholarly wisdom boasts not in its own achievements but in the Lord. This is why only the childlike have eyes to see God in his Word and in his world (Luke 10:21).[3]

Every level of mental life—from the most educated to the most uneducated—is fraught with the alluring power of living for the praise of man. The unique vulnerability of the intellectual elite is that the world buttresses this pride with extraordinary approval and esteem, while passing over the more low-brow forms of pride with less veneration.

One contemporary scholar shows how rampant this is among the faculties of many Christian colleges in the Christian College Coalition:

> Many of the Coalition faculty earn their doctorates at elite universities where little regard for faith, intellectual breadth, and Christian world-view is to be found. Consequently, one of the hallmarks of Coalition

---

[3] See chaps. 10–11.

faculty members, upon "returning" to the Christian college environment to teach, is not the aspiration to cultivate intellectual excellence for the glory of God so much as a deathly fear of being labeled "fundamentalist."[4]

Here we have a contemporary portrait of the difference between "the wise and understanding" and the "little children" mentioned in Luke 10:21.[5] The "little children" are little concerned with the praises of men and the human accolades for their intellectual work. They have been so humbled by the glory of God's grace and so satisfied by the beauty of God's greatness that all their energy aims at discovering more of God in his world and displaying what they have seen for others to see and enjoy. On the other hand, where there is the dread of belittling labels and "the ache . . . to be taken seriously in the unbelieving academy,"[6] we see the makings of "the wise and understanding" to whom God would not reveal his truth and glory.

Don't Leave the Path Because of Perils

But we have seen again and again that the perils that lurk on the path of serious thinking do not mean we should leave the path. There is no other path in the pursuit of knowing and loving God as fully as he would be known and loved. With all its perils, we must walk this path. We should not be so fearful that the task seems like a necessary evil. That is not the spirit of the Proverbs, which tell us to pursue the knowledge of God in his Word and in his world the way people seek silver and gold.

---

[4] J. Daryl Charles, "The Scandal of the Evangelical Mind" (A Forum of Responses), *First Things* 51 (March 1995): 38–39.

[5] See chap. 10.

[6] Douglas Wilson, "A Pauline Take on the New Perspective," *Credenda Agenda*, vol. 15, no. 5 (2003): p. 17. "The ache that some conservatives have to be taken seriously in the unbelieving academy is a pitiful thing indeed, and so I would like to take this opportunity to give the whole thing the universal raspberry. What Princeton, Harvard, Duke, and all the theological schools in Germany really need to hear is the horse-laugh of all Christendom. I mentioned earlier that proud flesh bonds to many strange things indeed, and I forgot to mention scholarship and footnotes. To steal a thought from Kierkegaard, 'Many scholars line their britches with journal articles festooned with footnotes in order to keep the Scriptures from spanking their academically-respectable pink, little bottoms.'"

Seek it like silver
>   and search for it as for hidden treasures. (Prov. 2:4)

Get wisdom,
>   and whatever you get, get insight. (Prov. 4:7)

Take my instruction instead of silver,
>   and knowledge rather than choice gold,
for wisdom is better than jewels,
>   and all that you may desire cannot compare with her. (Prov. 8:10–11)

How much better to get wisdom than gold!
>   To get understanding is to be chosen rather than silver. (Prov. 16:16)

Overall, Thinking Has Been Good for the Church

And lest we be so jaundiced in our suspicion of higher learning, Mark Noll reminds us in a balanced way that the path of serious thinking has, overall, been good for the church and the world.

> To be sure, hard intellectual labor has not always led to a healthy church. Sometimes, in fact, the pursuit of learning has been a means to escape the claims of the Gospel or the requirements of God's law. Yet, generally, the picture over the long term is different. Where Christian faith is securely rooted, where it penetrates deeply into a culture to change individual lives and redirect institutions, where it continues for more than a generation as a living testimony to the grace of God—in these situations, we almost invariably find Christians ardently cultivating the intellect for the glory of God.[7]

This has been the mind-set of the people whose shoulders we stand on today. They saw the implications of what it means that God reveals himself in history and in a Book. The history must be researched, and the Book must be read. Neither research nor reading is easy. But our forefathers believed the mental work was worth it.

---

[7]Mark Noll, "The Scandal of the Evangelical Mind," *Christianity Today* 37, no. 12 (October 25, 1993): p. 30.

> The Protestant Reformers, English Puritans, leaders of the 18th-century evangelical Awakenings like John Wesley and Jonathan Edwards, and a worthy line of stalwarts in the last century like Francis Asbury, Charles Hodge, and John Williamson Nevin—all believed that diligent, rigorous mental activity was a way to glorify God. None of them believed it was the only way, or even the highest way, but all believed in the life of the mind. And they believed in it because they were evangelical Christians.[8]

This mind-set is the reason that everywhere Christianity has spread, schools have spread. And the longer Christianity has stayed the more serious and thorough the educational enterprise has become. "During the Reformation, the major Protestants, especially Luther and Calvin, defended the absolute necessity for higher education against populist anti-intellectual movements. Invariably, where Protestant universities were strongest, the Protestant Reformation had its greatest impact."[9]

Neglect of Thinking in *This* World Is Folly

I share Noll's exuberance for the worth of Christian higher education, both because the Bible pushes us in that direction, and because this modern world calls for Christians to work out their faith in connection with serious thinking. Unlike the world of 250 years ago, the infrastructure of our society would collapse in a catastrophic way without hundreds of thousands of people who have been trained to think through extremely complex processes in creating, funding, manufacturing, managing, marketing, transporting, preserving, and disposing of tens of thousands of things we depend on every day. How does electricity get created and delivered to our homes? And how did all those electricity-dependent things (furnaces, lighting, refrigerators) come to be? In a world where rigorous thinking is woven into the fabric of life, the thought of *not* thinking seriously about God and his Word is folly.

---

[8]Ibid., 29.
[9]Ibid., 31.

Qualified Enthusiasm for Higher Learning

However, my enthusiasm for Christian scholarship is tempered by the realization of how relentlessly institutions of higher learning drift away from their allegiance to Christ and his Word. It is a sad tale.[10] Therefore it is salutary that Noll soberly confesses, "I do not think there is any future for Christian thinking from people who do not have an implicit, thorough trust in the truthfulness of the Bible."[11] He argues that the strategy of evangelicalism that will have the greatest impact for the glory of God in the modern world is "to embrace wholeheartedly a careful doctrine of inerrancy [of Scripture]."[12] It is only a starting point, but it is all-important. It undergirds the confidence that, in the Bible, we find the very words of God and his divine life through the gospel. "Nothing," Noll contends, "threatens evangelical Bible scholarship more than a denial of that life."[13]

When all the cautions have been heard—especially those concerning pride—the fact remains: God has revealed himself in his Word and in his world. He means to be known through the revelation of both, because he means to be loved fully. Moreover, when the psalmist ponders the place God has given to man in the created world, he marvels, "You have given him dominion over the works of your hands; you have put all things under his feet" (Ps. 8:6). Why has God done this? He did not do it to tempt us to idolatry by the beauty of what he has made. That came in with sin (Rom. 1:23). He did it because more of his glory would be known and treasured when seen through the prism of his creation.[14]

---

[10]See especially James Tunstead Burtchaell, *The Dying of the Light: The Disengagement of Colleges and Universities from Their Christian Churches* (Grand Rapids: Eerdmans, 1998). See also George Marsden, *The Soul of the American University: From Protestant Establishment to Established Nonbelief* (New York: Oxford University Press, 1994).

[11]Mark Noll, et al., "Scandal? A Forum on the Evangelical Mind," *Christianity Today* 39, no. 9 (August 14, 1995): p. 23.

[12]Mark Noll, *Between Faith and Criticism* (New York: Harper & Row, 1986), 196.

[13]Ibid., 197.

[14]I have tried to work out some of the practical implications of this for the ordinary Christian in "How to Wield the Word in the Fight for Joy: Using All Five Senses to See the Glory of God," in John Piper, *When I Don't Desire God: How to Fight for Joy* (Wheaton, IL: Crossway, 2004), 175–208.

All Knowing Is for the Love of God—Ours and Others'

All branches of learning exist ultimately for the purposes of knowing God, loving God, and loving man through Jesus. And since loving man means ultimately helping him see and savor God in Christ forever, it is profoundly right to say all thinking, all learning, all education, and all research is for the sake of knowing God, loving God, and showing God. "For from him and through him and to him are all things. To him be glory forever. Amen" (Rom. 11:36).

Encouraging Thinkers and Non-thinkers

Think over what I say,
for the Lord will give you understanding in everything.

2 Timothy 2:7

If you call out for insight
and raise your voice for understanding,
if you seek it like silver
and search for it as for hidden treasures,
then you will understand the fear of the Lord
and find the knowledge of God.
For the Lord gives wisdom;
from his mouth come knowledge and understanding.

Proverbs 2:3-6

Conclusion:
A Final Plea

In one sense the entire book is a plea. I said in the introduction that it is a plea to embrace serious thinking as a means of knowing and loving God and people. It is a plea to reject *either-or* thinking when it comes to head and heart, thinking and feeling, reason and faith, theology and doxology, mental labor and the ministry of love. But I do have some specific concluding pleas for two groups: those who love to think and those who don't. I promise not to scold or schmooze either group.

A Plea to Those Who Don't Love to Think

The first group is those of you who have little inclination to think about thinking. It's out of character that you are reading this, or that you even picked up the book. But strange things happen. These words may somehow have come into your hand. My plea is not that you get a different personality. Not everyone should be energized by the challenge of thinking. For you—and you are a very normal part of the great majority of human beings—my plea is fivefold.

1) *Be Thankful for Thinkers*

First, be humbly thankful for the countless benefits you enjoy both spiritually and naturally from those who have devoted their lives to the rigorous use of the mind. Without thousands of people who use their minds rigorously, you would not be wearing the clothes you have on, or driving the car you drive, or eating the food you eat, or holding a manufactured book in your hand.

You would not have a Bible without a long history of scholars who learned Greek and Hebrew, preserved the manuscripts, labored to keep available the original wording, and gave themselves to the exacting intellectual task of translating the Bible into a language you can read. If you find joy and help for your life in reading the Bible or hearing someone else read and teach it, you are standing on the shoulders of four thousand years of thinkers. I encourage you to be humbly thankful for them.

2) *Respect Those Who Serve You with Thinking*

Second, respect those who by inclination and calling devote time and effort to thinking for the sake of understanding the Bible and the world we live in. Christ has given pastors and teachers to the church (Eph. 4:11). Their job is to "labor in preaching and teaching" (1 Tim. 5:17), "rightly handling the word of truth" (2 Tim. 2:15), "able to give instruction in sound doctrine and also to rebuke those who contradict it" (Titus 1:9). That is not all they do. But this part of their life is difficult, important, and precious. Respect them for their work. As Paul says, "Respect those who labor among you . . . esteem them very highly in love because of their work" (1 Thess. 5:12–13).

3) *Pray for the Vulnerable Thinkers*

Third, pray earnestly for the teachers and preachers and scholars in the churches and the seminaries and colleges. I share the dismay at how often intellectual leaders depart from the Scriptures and lead people astray. But too seldom do we pray for them. I pray regularly for some influential scholars in the hope that they will experience such an encounter with God in his Word that they will forsake what they have taught for decades and embrace what the Bible really teaches. I invite you to join me.[1]

---

[1] For my suggestion on how to pray for the seminaries and colleges, see John Piper, "Brothers, Pray for the Seminaries," in *Brothers, We Are Not Professionals* (Nashville: Broadman, 2002), 261–66, or see the online version: http://www.desiringgod.org/ResourceLibrary/Articles/ByDate/1995/1565.

4) *Avoid Wrongheaded Thinking*

Fourth, even though you don't often think about the way you think, try to avoid the worst mental mistakes in dealing with the Bible and those who teach it. For example, if you are listening to a preacher and he says something like, "God can't be completely sovereign and yet humans still be responsible for their choices," don't suddenly jump on that misguided intellectual train. Instead say to him, "Sure he can; both are in the Bible." Then go on about your work.

5) *Read Your Bible with Joy*

Fifth, even though you are not self-conscious of your thought processes and see yourself as just an ordinary reader of the Bible, don't let anything I say keep you from doing that more and more. The truth you see in the Bible by God's grace will be your life. You don't have to be a scholar. You don't even have to be aware that you are thinking when you read. You *are* thinking when you read. But you don't have to think about it.

It will be helpful from time to time to make sure that your un-self-conscious thinking is not leading you astray. That's what pastors and teachers and books are for. But, in general, just keep reading the Bible. Memorize it. Enjoy it. See Christ everywhere in it.[2] Treasure him more and more. And apply the Bible to your life—all of your life.

A Plea to Those Who Love to Think

The second group of people I have in mind are those who love to think. Figuring things out is your joy. Some of you are more analytical. You like to take things apart and see how they work. Others of you like to put things together into coherent structures. Many of you like to do both. I have written this book to bless you. I want to encourage you that your bent is needed and that there is an important place for

---

[2]For my effort to show how all the Scriptures relate to Jesus, see "If You Believed Moses, You Would Believe Me, for He Wrote of Me" (sermon on John 5:33–47), October 4, 2009, http://www.desiringGod.org.

you in the church and in the world. I want to inspire you to pursue the use of your mind to know God and love people. So, for you I have a fourfold plea.

1) *Think Consciously for the Glory of Christ*

First, make all your thinking a partner in God's ultimate purpose to magnify the supreme worth of his glory—the glory of Christ. This is the ultimate theme and purpose of Scripture. This is why all thinking and all scholarship exists. The heavens are designed by God to tell the glory of God (Ps. 19:1; Rom. 1:19–21; Col. 1:16); Pharaoh and every human king exists for the glory of God (Ex. 9:16; Acts 12:23); all of redemptive history exists for the praise of his glory (Eph. 1:6); everything you do, from eating to dying, is to be for his glory (1 Cor. 10:31; John 21:19); history will end with everyone marveling at his glory (2 Thess. 1:10). Make God's supreme beauty and worth the driving force of all your thinking. And make it the centerpiece of everything you create.

2) *Become like Children*

Second, humble yourself under the mighty hand of God. "Unless you turn and become like children, you will never enter the kingdom of heaven" (Matt. 18:3). Of course, as we have seen, Jesus did not mean that we are to think at the level of a third-grader. He meant, be humble and dependent. "Do not be children in your thinking. Be infants in evil, but in your thinking be mature" (1 Cor. 14:20). Humility is the great prerequisite for understanding the truth of God—and that means the truth that matters most about everything.

Admit and confess your absolute dependence on Christ and his Spirit. "Apart from me you can do nothing" (John 15:5). Without Christ and his death on your behalf, you would still be under the wrath of God (John 3:36; Rom. 8:3; Gal. 3:13). But because of Christ, God is for us. And if God is for us, who can be against us? "All are yours . . . and you are Christ's, and Christ is God's" (1 Cor. 3:22–23).

This should make you humble, not cocky. The Corinthian thinkers got this wrong. And Paul had to remind them, "What do you have that you did not receive? If then you received it, why do you boast as if you did not receive it?" (1 Cor. 4:7). Seek understanding like silver. Not because in the end it depends on you, but because in the end God is gracious. Lay hold of every treasure because he has laid hold of you (Phil. 3:12).

Beware of showing off. (I'm still pleading for your humility.) Thinkers are often clever folks. Therefore, I plead with you to keep in mind the crucial word from James Denney: "No man can give the impression that he himself is clever and that Christ is mighty to save."[3] The temptation is huge in our day among very gifted entertainment-oriented preachers. They make a trademark out of clever speech. There is, from time to time, a place for the shrewd and penetrating riposte, but as a diet, it does not magnify Christ or feed the soul.

3) *Enjoy the Word of God like Gold and Honey*

Third, delight yourself in the Word of God day and night. Yes, thinking is often hard work. That's why Paul said, "Do your best to present yourself to God as one approved, *a worker* who has no need to be ashamed, rightly handling the word of truth" (2 Tim. 2:15). *Worker* is the right word. But it is not the only word. I am pleading with you to delight in the Word of God. "His *delight* is in the law of the LORD, and on his law he meditates day and night" (Ps. 1:2). "The precepts of the LORD are right, *rejoicing* the heart. . . . More to be desired are they than gold, even much fine gold; sweeter also than honey and drippings of the honeycomb" (Ps. 19:8, 10). "Your words were found, and I ate them, and your words became to me a joy and the delight of my heart" (Jer. 15:16).

I am pleading that in all your thinking you seek to see and savor

---

[3]Quoted in John Stott, *Between Two Worlds: The Art of Preaching in the Twentieth Century* (Grand Rapids: Eerdmans, 1982), 325.

the Treasure. If thinking has the reputation of being only emotion-less logic, all will be in vain. God did not give us minds as ends in themselves. The mind provides the kindling for the fires of the heart. Theology serves doxology. Reflection serves affection. Contemplation serves exultation. Together they glorify Christ to the full.

4) *Think for the Sake of Love*

Fourth, make all your thinking an act of love for people. "Let all that you do be done in love" (1 Cor. 16:14)—that includes thinking. "The aim of our charge is love" (1 Tim. 1:5)—that charge includes, "Think over what I say" (2 Tim. 2:7). "If I . . . understand all mysteries and all knowledge . . . but have not love, I am nothing" (1 Cor. 13:2).

Thinking that does not aim to display Christ and build up people is not worthy of God's approval. It may produce wonders—antibiot-ics, buildings, bridges, books, big-screen TVs—but the final stamp on the box will be: Disapproved. For "whatever does not proceed from faith is sin. . . . Without faith it is impossible to please [God]" (Rom. 14:23; Heb. 11:6).

A Gift of Grace, and a Pathway to More

I end with one last reminder of the two passages of Scripture that contain the main point of this book. Paul's word to Timothy: "Think over what I say, for the Lord will give you understanding in every-thing" (2 Tim. 2:7). And the plea of Proverbs: "If you call out for insight and raise your voice for understanding, if you seek it like silver and search for it as for hidden treasures, then you will under-stand the fear of the LORD and find the knowledge of God. For the LORD gives wisdom; from his mouth come knowledge and under-standing" (Prov. 2:3–6).

We think, and the Lord *gives* understanding. We seek it like sil-ver; the Lord *gives* it. Not *either-or*. *Both-and*. Our thinking does not replace God's grace. It is the gift of grace and the pathway to more and more.

Appendix 1
"The Earth Is the Lord's":
The Supremacy of Christ in Christian Learning
Biblical Foundations for Bethlehem College and Seminary[1]

This is a message I delivered on November 5, 2008, at Bethlehem
Baptist Church to mark the creation of Bethlehem College and
Seminary. I include it here as an example of how the aim of this book
might find expression in the vision for a new school.

First, a few comments about the spirit from which this vision of
Bethlehem College and Seminary flows. There is no sense of trium-
phalism here. There is no sense of having the last word in education,
or easy answers to the challenges of our times, or the ideal philosophy of college and seminary training.

Instead, there is a trembling sense that pride and poverty (and
many other things!) make this a dangerous undertaking. A word
about each of these.

The Danger of Pride

One of the most fertile fields of pride is academic higher education.
I spent sixteen years of my life in it and have felt its dangers. And I

---

[1] What do we mean by the terms *college* and *seminary*? We simply mean that as soon as feasible, we
will offer an accredited Bachelor of Arts and Master of Divinity. The words *college* and *seminary* do
not signify hundreds of students, or multiple academic departments, or large faculties, or athletic
teams. Instead, in the *seminary*, think of a group of a dozen students or so (nowadays called a *cohort*)
linked with pastoral mentors, moving together through the unified course sequence based on the
Greek and Hebrew Bible.

And in the *college*, think similarly of a cohort of students moving together through an inte-
grated and unified curriculum of humanities and sciences built into a historical framework from
creation to the present. Think Bethlehem faculty mentors and many guest professors. Think of
both these programs as church-based, where all the students are expected to be involved in the life
and ministry of the church. Our aim is that the limited scope of the programs, and the connection
with the church, and the wider funding of the vision will bring down costs to the place where students will not be burdened with debt when they are finished. The present financial crisis in higher
education is one of the reasons for starting Bethlehem College and Seminary, but not the main one.

read this morning in Ezekiel 16 how God took Israel from her misery and made her beautiful and renowned. Then the dreadful verse 15 said, "But you trusted in your beauty and played the whore because of your renown."

And I thought, God has blessed Bethlehem and The Bethlehem Institute and Desiring God and me personally. And the greatest danger of all right now is that we trust in our blessed condition and our renown. Pride lurks at every door. So we tremble and ask, "Is this our motive—to flaunt power, to get praise, to make a name for ourselves?" If so, oh God, may we fail, and fail quickly without harming others.

But pride has other forms, and one is cowardice—the fear of being criticized. And criticism there will be aplenty, because this school will affirm biblical truths that are unpopular, even with many Christians, as beautiful as we think they are (I will mention ten of them later on). That is the risk we believe we are called to take. And may the Lord do whatever it takes to keep us humble and make us servants, not lords, as we move forward with Bethlehem College and Seminary.

The Danger of Poverty

Another reality that makes a college and seminary a dangerous undertaking is that, as we read our books and listen to our lectures and write our papers and have our discussions, we are aware that our urban centers are broken and generations languish unable to escape the tangles of addiction and dysfunction and poverty and crime. And beyond these shores are millions of people who live with no clean water, insufficient food, and no medical care, and who could only dream of such an education. This vast discrepancy gives us a sense of uneasiness in the affluent halls of learning.

But then we ask, "Is the answer to the miseries of the world a generation of young people who do not know how to observe accurately, or think carefully, or know history, or understand culture, or comprehend the Bible, or plan strategically?" So again we take the risk and pray that Bethlehem College and Seminary will not be part of the problem of poverty but part of the solution. We pray that because students will develop habits of mind and heart that will move them toward need, not comfort.

Biblical Foundations

We turn now to the biblical foundations of Bethlehem College and Seminary. In 1 Corinthians 10:25–26 the apostle Paul said, "Eat whatever is sold in the meat market without raising any question on the ground of conscience. For 'the earth is the Lord's, and the fullness thereof.'" This implies Jesus Christ owns the world and everything in it. It also implies that we who are his loyal subjects may make use of any of it freely for his glory. Education is about how we do that.

Abraham Kuyper, who founded the Free University of Amsterdam in 1880, said in one of his most famous sentences, "No single piece of our mental world is to be hermetically sealed off from the rest, and there is not a square inch in the whole domain of our human existence over which Christ, who is Sovereign over all, does not cry, 'Mine!'"[2] This was the foundation of his educational dream for the Free University.

That truth is absolutely biblical and true and foundational to Bethlehem College and Seminary, but it is not the most ultimate or defining truth. Christ not only made and owns the world, he not only holds everything together by the word of his power, but he also created it and sustains it to display his beauty and his worth and greatness so that those whom he created in his image will know him and treasure him above all things, and in that treasuring of him above all that he has made, manifest his supreme value in the universe. That's the ultimately defining truth for Bethlehem College and Seminary. The decisive text in this regard is Colossians 1:15–17:

---

[2]Abraham Kuyper, *Abraham Kuyper: A Centennial Reader*, ed. James D. Bratt (Grand Rapids: Eerdmans, 1998), 488.

> [Christ] is the image of the invisible God, the firstborn of all creation.
> For by him all things were created, in heaven and on earth, visible and
> invisible, whether thrones or dominions or rulers or authorities—all
> things were created through him and *for him*. And he is before all
> things, and in him all things hold together.

So we learn that Christ made all things and holds all things together
"for himself." "All things were created through him and *for him*." "For
him" does not mean that Christ had deficiencies that he had to create
the world to supply. It means that his complete self-sufficiency over-
flowed in the creation of the world so that the world would display
the greatness of Christ.

That is the deepest foundation stone of Bethlehem College and
Seminary. All things not only *belong to* Christ, but all things *display*
Christ. Human beings exist to magnify his worth in the world.
Our worth consists of our capacity to consciously make much of
his worth. The goal of Bethlehem College and Seminary cannot be
expressed with man as the end point. Christ is the end point. All
things are "from him and through him and to him" (Rom. 11:36).
"Not to us, O Lord, not to us, but to your name give glory" (Ps. 115:1).

No paragraph outside the Bible is more foundational to this
school than one from the notebooks of Jonathan Edwards. It not only
sums up the ultimate purpose of God to glorify himself in creation
but also shows how God accomplishes that self-exaltation in such a
way that it becomes love and not megalomania. Here is how Edwards
says it, and with this he opens the door for Bethlehem College and
Seminary to be unshakably joyful and radically God-exalting in the
very same act:

> God glorifies himself towards the creatures also [in] two ways: (1) by
> appearing to . . . their understanding; (2) in communicating himself
> to their hearts, and in their rejoicing and delighting in, and enjoying
> the manifestations which he makes of himself. . . . *God is glorified not
> only by his glory's being seen, but by its being rejoiced in*. . . . [W]hen those
> that see it delight in it: God is more glorified than if they only see it; his

glory is then received by the whole soul, both by the understanding and by the heart. . . . He that testifies his idea of God's glory [doesn't] glorify God so much as he that testifies also his approbation of it and his delight in it.[3]

Essential to the foundation of Bethlehem College and Seminary is the truth that God is most glorified in us when we are most satisfied in him. God's self-exaltation and our everlasting joy are not at odds. They happen together. His worth is magnified when we treasure him above all things. Our joy in him reflects his glory. The great quest of Bethlehem College and Seminary is for minds and hearts that see and savor the glory of Christ in all things and spread that experience to the world.[4]

Everywhere you turn in the history of redemption, from beginning to end, God's design is the same: that his glory—supremely the glory of his grace in the person and work of Christ—be seen and savored and spread. God is manifestly exuberant about making himself and his Son supreme in the thoughts and affections of his people and making himself known as Lord in the world.

That is the ultimate foundation of why Christ is supreme in Christian learning and in Bethlehem College and Seminary. We are

---

[3]Jonathan Edwards, "Miscellanies," ed. Thomas Schafer, *The Works of Jonathan Edwards*, vol. 13 (New Haven, CT: Yale University Press, 1994), 495 (Miscellany 448) emphasis added.

[4]I have laid out the biblical foundation for this more fully in several places. See for example, *Let the Nations Be Glad*, 3rd ed. (Grand Rapids: Baker Academic, 2010), 39–46, and *The Pleasures of God* (Sisters, OR: Multnomah, 2000), chaps. 1 and 4. The ultimate biblical foundation for the truth that we glorify God by joining him joyfully in his goal to glorify himself in all things is that God does indeed make himself the supreme goal of all that he does in the world from beginning to end. We are not the main point of the universe. God is.

- He created us for his glory: "Bring my sons from afar and my daughters from the end of the earth, . . . whom I *created for my glory*, whom I formed and made" (Isa. 43:6–7).
- Christ will come again at the end of the age for his glory: "*He comes on that day to be glorified* in his saints, and *to be marveled* at among all who have believed" (2 Thess. 1:9–10).
- Romans 9:23 says that all his mercy, all his wrath, and all his power are aiming "*to make known the riches of his glory* for vessels of mercy, which he has prepared beforehand for glory."
- In 1 Corinthians 10:31, God makes himself the aim of every human endeavor from the smallest to the largest: "So, whether you eat or drink, or whatever you do, *do all to the glory of God*."
- In Romans 3:23, God defines the very essence of sin as failing to make him supreme: "For all have sinned and *fall short of the glory of God*." Sin is sin because it belittles the glory of God.
- And when God's act of redemption reaches its climactic moment in the death of Christ for sinners, the aim of God is that the glory of his grace be seen and praised above all things: "He predestined us for adoption as sons through Jesus Christ, according to the purpose of his will, *to the praise of his glorious grace*" (Eph. 1:5–6). And he defined the gospel in 2 Corinthians 4:4 as "the light of *the gospel of the glory of Christ*, who is the image of God."

simply joining God himself in his exuberant commitment to magnify his greatness and the glory of his Son.

What Do We Study?

The question arises: "Where do we see his glory?" That is, what is the focus of our education? What do we study? If God's aim in creating and governing the world is the display of his glory that we might see it and delight in it and reflect it, where will we focus our attention? Where will we see it? How does this happen?

The answer is that God has two books: the Word and the world—the Bible, on the one hand, and the whole organic complex of nature and history and human culture, on the other hand. The Bible is inspired and authoritative. The world is not. But this doesn't mean that all we focus on is the Bible. The Bible gives the decisive meaning of all things. But the Bible itself sends us over and over again to the world for learning. Consider the lilies; consider the birds (Matt. 6:26, 28). "Go to the ant, O sluggard; consider her ways, and be wise" (Prov. 6:6). "The heavens declare the glory of God, and the sky above proclaims his handiwork" (Ps. 19:1). "Lift up your eyes on high and see: who created these?" (Isa. 40:26).

In fact, think about the way the prophets and apostles and Jesus himself used language. They used analogies and figures and metaphors and similes and illustrations and parables. They constantly assume that we have looked at the world and learned about vineyards, wine, weddings, lions, bears, horses, dogs, pigs, grasshoppers, constellations, businesses, wages, banks, fountains, springs, rivers, fig trees, olive trees, mulberry trees, thorns, wind, thunderstorms, bread, baking, armies, swords, shields, sheep, shepherds, cattle, camels, fire, green wood, dry wood, hay, stubble, jewels, gold, silver, law courts, judges, and advocates.

In other words, the Bible both commands and assumes that we will know the *world* and not just the *Word*. We will study the *general* book of God called *nature and history and culture*. And we will study the *special* book of God called *the Bible*. And the reason is that God has revealed his glory in both—and means for us to see him in both.

The two books of God are not on the same level. The Bible has supreme authority, because God gave the Bible as the key to unlock the meaning of all things. Without the truth of the Bible, the most brilliant scholars may learn amazing things about nature. And we may read their books and learn from them. But they miss the main point without the special revelation of God—that everything exists to glorify Christ, that they are blinded by sin, that they need a Savior, that Christ came into the world to save sinners, and that the whole universe gets its ultimate meaning in relationship to him. When they miss the main thing, everything is skewed.

So the entire curriculum of Bethlehem College and Seminary is permeated by the study of the Bible. The Bible gives the key that unlocks the deepest meaning of everything else.[5]

What Do We Do with God's Books?

So if Bethlehem College and Seminary is going to focus on these two books—the Word that God inspired and the world that God made—because this is where God has revealed his glory, then what should we do with these two books? What does this education try to impart to the students?

Our aim is not to impart degrees. The BA and MDiv degrees are almost entirely incidental to the aims of education.

Our aim is not mainly to impart facts because these will be soon forgotten, but the aims of education should last.

Our aim is not mainly to impart skills for a trade or a profession, since these change with the trades and technologies.

Our aim is to build into the student habits of mind and heart that will never leave them and will fit them for a lifetime of ongoing growth. The well-educated person is the person who has the habits

---

[5]See John Piper, "Thoughts on the Sufficiency of Scripture," at http://www.desiringgod.org/ResourceLibrary/TasteAndSee/ByDate/2005/1282.

of mind and heart to go on learning what he needs to learn to live in a Christ-exalting way for the rest of his life—and that would apply to whatever sphere of life he pursues.

These habits of mind apply to all objects in the world but most importantly to the Bible. We can sum them up like this:

> We aim to enable and to motivate the student to *observe* his subject matter accurately and thoroughly, to *understand* clearly what he has observed, to *evaluate* fairly what he has understood by deciding what is true and valuable, to *feel* intensely according to the value of what he has evaluated, to *apply* wisely and helpfully in life what he understands and feels, and to *express* in speech and writing and deeds what he has seen, understood, felt, and applied in such a way that its accuracy, clarity, truth, value, and helpfulness can be known and enjoyed by others.

So the habits of mind and heart are:

- observing
- understanding
- evaluating
- feeling
- applying
- expressing

Whether you are looking at a passage in the Bible, or at the U.S. Constitution, or at a mysterious pattern of scratches on your car, the habits of mind and heart are the same.

1) Observing

We aim to enable and to motivate the student to *observe* his subject matter accurately and thoroughly. We must see what is really there. Our teaching is designed to force students to see for themselves. They must keep looking until they see things they did not see at first—in the Word and in the world.

We must learn to read slowly and observe rigorously and comprehensively and with a view to details. The observing must be accurate and thorough. Otherwise, our understanding and evaluation will be flawed. Quickly reading *many* books ordinarily begets bad habits of mind. We will not encourage students to read for the sake of quantity but to read with rigorous observation and reflection.

2) Understanding

We aim to enable and to motivate the student to understand clearly what he has observed thoroughly and accurately. Understanding involves the severe discipline of thinking. The mind wrestles with the traits and features of what it has observed. The aim when reading the Bible is that we discern the mind of God through what the biblical authors intended us to understand. This understanding comes through the language conventions on the page. We observe them and we think about them until we can say, "I understand what he meant." We want *his*, not ours. We aim to think the author's thoughts after him. Otherwise, education simply becomes a reflection of our own ignorance.

3) Evaluating

We aim to enable and to motivate the student to evaluate fairly but not to shrink back from the judgments that must be made about truth and value on the basis of careful observation and accurate understanding. Here is where our worldview will make all the difference. We believe there is such a thing as truth and that with the compass of the Scriptures and the help of the Spirit, we can know it.

4) Feeling

We aim to enable and to motivate the student to feel properly in response to what he has observed and understood and evaluated. His feeling should be in accord with the truth and worth of what he has observed and understood. If he has observed and understood a terrible reality like hell, his feelings should be fear and horror and compassion. If he has observed and understood a wonderful reality like heaven, then his feelings should be joy and hope and longing.

Albert Einstein's indictment of preachers illustrates what I am trying to say. Charles Misner, a scientific specialist in general relativity theory, was quoted this way:

> I do see the design of the universe as essentially a religious question. That is, one should have some kind of respect and awe for the whole business. . . . It's very magnificent and shouldn't be taken for granted. In fact, I believe that is why Einstein had so little use for organized religion, although he strikes me as a basically very religious man. *He must have looked at what the preachers said about God and felt that they were blaspheming. He had seen much more majesty than they had ever imagined, and they were just not talking about the real thing.* My guess is that he simply felt that religions he'd run across did not have proper respect . . . for the author of the universe.[6]

This is devastating, because I cannot imagine that from our vantage point sixty years later preachers would seem to Einstein any more moved by greatness than they did then.

What's wrong? There is a disconnect between the greatness of God and the emotional response of the preachers. To Einstein it looked as if they were not "talking about the real thing." It felt so out of proportion to Einstein that it seemed like they were blaspheming. In other words, if here is a God of the sort that Christians say they believe in, you have dealings with him and respond as unemotionally as that.

Scientists know that light travels at the speed of 5.87 trillion miles a year. They also know the galaxy of which our solar system is a part is about 100,000 light-years in diameter—about 587 thousand trillion miles. It is one of about a million such galaxies in the optical range of our most powerful telescopes. In our galaxy there are about one hundred billion stars. The sun is one of them, a modest star burning at about 6,000 degrees centigrade on the surface

---

[6]Quoted in *First Things* 18 (Dec. 1991): 63 (italics added).

and traveling in an orbit at 155 miles per second, which means it will take about two hundred million years to complete a revolution around the galaxy.

Scientists know these things. Einstein was awed by them. He felt something like this: "If there is a personal God, as the Christians say, who spoke this universe into being, then there is a certain respect and reverence and wonder and dread that would have to come through when we talk about him. And certainly we would be talking about him all the time since he is the most important reality." You can feel the force of this when you hear God say in Isaiah 40:25–26:

> "To whom will you compare me?
>> Or who is my equal?" says the Holy One.
> Lift your eyes and look to the heavens:
>> Who created all these [stars]?
> He who brings out the starry host one by one,
> and calls them each by name.
> Because of his great power and mighty strength,
> not one of them is missing. (NIV)

Every one of the billions of stars in the universe is there by God's specific appointment. He knows their number. And most astonishing of all, he knows them by name. By name! They do his bidding as if they were his personal agents.

Einstein felt some of this, and his response was: Christian preachers are just not talking about the real thing. What's wrong is that the supremacy of God is not a *heartfelt* experience in most Christian preaching.

Since God is glorified in our emotional response to his glory and not just by seeing it and understanding it and evaluating it, we cannot be indifferent to the emotional life of the students. This means that prayer, and reliance on the Holy Spirit, and the cultivating of a sense of wonder become essential in the life of Bethlehem College and Seminary.

5) Applying

We aim to enable and to motivate the student to apply wisely and helpfully what he has observed and understood and evaluated and felt. It takes wisdom, not just factual knowledge, to know how to wisely and helpfully apply what he understands and feels.

If students observed and understood and felt the truth that they should "redeem the time" (from Eph. 5:16), a wise application might be go to bed earlier and get up earlier so that there is time for devotions without being exhausted. Or it might be to get a job as an intern at an inner-city emergency service center. A well-educated person is growing in the wise application to life of all he learns.

6) Expressing

We aim to enable and to motivate the student to express in speech and writing and deeds what he has seen, understood, evaluated, felt, and applied. And the goal is that he do it in such a way that its accuracy, clarity, truthfulness, preciousness, and helpfulness can be known and enjoyed by others. We want the students to have a growing ability to communicate and demonstrate compellingly to others what they have seen and understood and evaluated and felt and applied.

We live in a day that is not congenial to accuracy and precision in public discourse. Language is seen more as a tool for creating desired effects than for transmitting truth clearly. "Spin" has a meaning today that it did not have fifty years ago. The way language is used today is often contrary to the standards that the apostle Paul set for himself:

> We have renounced disgraceful, underhanded ways. We refuse to practice cunning or to *tamper with God's word*, but *by the open statement of the truth* we would commend ourselves to everyone's conscience *in the sight of God.* . . . For we are not, like so many, *peddlers of God's word*, but as men of sincerity, as commissioned by God, *in the sight of God we speak* in Christ. (2 Cor. 4:2; 2:17)

This is not what is happening when Bill Clinton, on his way to his party's nomination for president, said in a speech, "Scripture says: 'Our eyes have not seen, nor our ears heard nor our minds imagined what we can build.'" This was an allusion to 1 Corinthians 2:9–10: "What no eye has seen, nor ear heard, nor the heart of man imagined, what God has prepared for those who love him." When I heard Clinton's quotation, I felt a sense of dismay that God's Word could be so manipulated.

And to make sure you know this is a nonpartisan critique, it got no better when President George H. W. Bush, at the 1992 National Religious Broadcasters gathering, said in defense of the Gulf War, "I want to thank you for helping America, as Christ ordained, to be a light unto the world." This is an allusion to Matthew 5:14—"You are the light of the world"—which, of course, was not about America but about the followers of Christ.

This is the kind of peddling of God's Word that Paul rejected. Words in the Bible have a meaning fixed by the intention of God, expressed through the mind of the human authors. It cannot be made to mean what we choose without tampering with God's Word. But the atmosphere of our time puts so little premium on truth that the language of the Bible and of historical Christian documents has become a wax nose to shape according to the desires of the speaker.

This is not new. At the Council of Nicaea in AD 325 the Arians were fighting to defend their view that Jesus Christ was not equally divine with God the Father and that he had a beginning. When Scriptures were used by those defending his deity, strangely the Arians accepted them. Only when terms were found that removed all ambiguity could the council really know what the Arians were affirming. Here is how Gregory of Nazianzus described the event:

> The Alexandrians . . . confronted the Arians with the traditional Scriptural phrases which appeared to leave no doubt as to the eternal Godhead of the Son. But to their surprise they were met with perfect acquiescence. Only as each test was propounded, it was observed that

the suspected party whispered and gesticulated to one another, evidently hinting that each could be safely accepted, since it admitted of evasion. . . . The fathers were baffled, and the test of *homoousion* [an interpretive Greek phrase meaning "of one nature" with the Father] . . . was being forced upon the majority by the evasions of the Arians.[7]

Imprecision and vagueness have been used for thousands of years by those who want to abandon meanings and retain words. J. Gresham Machen, one of the founders of Westminster Theological Seminary, saw it in the early part of the twentieth century and described it like this in relation to the doctrinal defections of the Presbyterian church:

This temper of mind is hostile to precise definitions. Indeed nothing makes a man more unpopular in the controversies of the present day than an insistence upon definitions of terms. . . . Men discourse very eloquently today upon such subjects as God, religion, Christianity, atonement, redemption, faith; but are greatly incensed when they are asked to tell in simple language what they mean by these terms.[8]

Our aim at Bethlehem College and Seminary is to cultivate habits of the heart and mind that help students express the truth they have discovered so that its accuracy, clarity, truthfulness, preciousness, and helpfulness are manifest. Together with the apostle Paul we renounce linguistic cunning. We turn from any tampering with God's Word. We embrace the integrity of "the open statement of the truth." We speak before the face of God and for the glory of the God of truth.

This brings us back to our original reason for being. God created the world and inspired the Word to display his glory. A well-educated person sees the glory of God in the inspired Word of God and in the created world of God, and understands it and evaluates it and feels it and applies it and expresses it for others to see and enjoy.

---

[7]Gregory of Nazianzus, *Oration 21: On Athanasius of Alexandria*, in "Gregory Nazianzus, Select Orations, Sermons, Letters; Dogmatic Treatises," in *Nicene and Post-Nicene Fathers*, vol. 7, 2nd Series, ed. P. Shaff and H. Wace (repr. Grand Rapids: Eerdmans, 1955), 171–72.

[8]J. Gresham Machen, *What Is Faith?* (1937; repr. Edinburgh: Banner of Truth, 1991), 13–14.

Where We Stand

We do not assume that the process of deciding what is true and valuable starts over with every generation of students. And it didn't start with us. Therefore, we are a confessional institution. The Bethlehem Elder Affirmation of Faith[9] defines what we believe and teach in Bethlehem College and Seminary.

We do not aim to force students into this mold. That would not be education, not an honor to Christ. We aim to come alongside them in the processes of observation, understanding, evaluation, feeling, application, and expression and show them why we land where we do. The faculty will advocate and seek to persuade. We will not coerce or deceive or hide difficult problems. In this way, we believe truth will be honored, and the integrity of careful thinking will be encouraged.

We believe that this way of doing education—with a view to seeing and savoring and spreading the glory of Christ, while making his Word our supreme rule in all our thinking about his world, with these rigorous habits of mind and heart—leads to humble, courageous convictions in a fallen world where Christ urges us to live peaceably as far as it lies in us (Rom. 12:18), but not to shrink back from telling the truth that is often controversial (Matt. 10:27–28; Acts 20:20, 27).

Therefore, I pray that Bethlehem College and Seminary will be marked by unashamed courage and openness in the stands we take. We feel the force of this quote, often attributed to Martin Luther,[10] as it relates to the controversies of our day:

> If I profess with the loudest voice and clearest exposition every portion of the truth of God except precisely that little point which the world and the devil are at that moment attacking, I am not confessing Christ, however boldly I may be professing Christ. Where the battle rages there

---

[9]You can read the Bethlehem Elder Affirmation of Faith at http://www.hopeingod.org/document/elder-affirmation-faith.

[10]Denny Burk argues that the quotation may not in fact be from Luther: http://www.dennyburk.com/the-apocryphal-martin-luther.

the loyalty of the soldier is proved, and to be steady on all the battle-field besides is mere flight and disgrace if he flinches at that point.[11]

It will be helpful in closing to position Bethlehem College and Seminary in such battles. Here are a few, with the battleground in bold and our position following.

1) **Historical criticism.** *The Bible teaches only what is true. It is coherent and non-contradictory in the progress of revelation.*

The Bible is inspired and inerrant so that what it teaches is true and stands in judgment on all tradition and all science and all culture and all human opinion. It is more precious than gold and sweeter than honey. It is worthy of a lifetime of assiduous reflection, heart-felt meditation, and joyful obedience.

2) **Roman Catholicism.** *Justification involves the imputation of Christ's righteousness by faith alone.*

Justification by grace alone through faith alone on the basis of Christ alone for the glory of God alone is at the heart of the biblical gospel. It includes the imputation, not the impartation, of the righteousness of Christ to us and on the basis of Christ's perfect obedience to all that the Father commanded him to do.

3) **Relativism and pluralism.** *Jesus is the only way to God.*

In order to be saved from eternal damnation, all peoples—Jewish and Muslim and Hindu and Buddhist and animist and secularist—must know and believe in Jesus Christ as the Lord and Savior who died for them and rose again. World missions is a priority for all who love people, know Christ, and see the world of unreached peoples.

---

[11]Quoted in Parker T. Williamson, *Standing Firm: Reclaiming Christian Faith in Times of Controversy* (Springfield, PA: PLC Publications, 1996), 5.

4) **Universalism and annihilationism.** *Hell is real and terrible.*

Hell, as Jesus taught more than anyone else, is real. It is a conscious, eternal experience of torment pictured in part as weeping and gnashing of teeth, outer darkness, unquenchable fire, eternal punishment, divine vengeance, and the lake of fire. People should be warned with tears and urgency.

5) **Abortion.** *The unfettered abortion license is abominable.*

Abortion is morally monstrous. Unborn human life should be protected for the same reasons that all human life should be protected.

6) **Feminism and egalitarianism.** *The complementary differences of manhood and womanhood are beautiful, practical, and important.*

Concerning biblical manhood and womanhood we believe that God's merciful purpose for our great good is that humble, Christlike, servant-hearted men bear the burden of leadership as elders and pastors in the church and that such men function as the caring, providing, protecting leaders of their homes; and that women come alongside these men with their manifold gifts and help them carry through the mission of the church and the home.

7) **Divorce and homosexuality.** *Marriage is a lifelong covenant between a man and a woman.*

No kind of relationship between two men or two women is marriage. Whatever two men do or say to each other, or whatever two women do or say to each other, it is not now, never has been, and never will be marriage in God's eyes. Marriage is the lifelong covenant relationship between a man and a woman as husband and wife on the analogy of Christ and the church.

8) **Racism and ethnocentrism.** *Delighting in and desiring racial and ethnic diversity is crucial.*

Indifference to active love across ethnic lines is an assault on the purpose of the cross of Christ who ransomed people from every tribe and tongue and people and nation. Happy, unified ethnic diversity in Christ is our destiny in the age to come and should be loved, longed for, and sought after here and now.

9) **Consumerism and materialism.** *Desiring riches is deadly, and wartime simplicity is good.*

Desiring to be rich is suicidal, and commending that desire as part of the Christian life is therefore worse than murderous because not just this life but the next is at stake. Followers of Jesus should feel a magnetic pull on their lives toward wartime simplicity so that they may be lavish in giving and alleviate as much suffering as they can—especially eternal suffering.

10) **Arminianism and open theism.**[12] *God is absolutely sovereign.*

God is sovereign over all things including natural calamity and human sin. To quote the Bethlehem Elder Affirmation of Faith:

> God, from all eternity, in order to display the full extent of His glory for the eternal and ever-increasing enjoyment of all who love Him, did, by the most wise and holy counsel of His will, freely and unchangeably ordain and foreknow whatever comes to pass. God upholds and governs all things—from galaxies to subatomic particles, from the forces of nature to the movements of nations, and from the public plans of politicians to the secret acts of solitary persons—all in accord with His eternal, all-wise purposes to glorify Himself, yet in such a way that He never sins, nor ever condemns a person unjustly; but that His ordain-

---

[12]Classical Arminianism is not the same as open theism. Open theism argues that if man is to have free will understood as ultimate self-determination, then he must be able to create choices that God cannot foresee. Therefore, God does not have exhaustive knowledge of what will come to pass. Arminianism, while granting that meaning of free will, does not draw that conclusion about God's foreknowledge.

ing and governing all things is compatible with the moral account-ability of all persons created in His image.

For Our Joy, to His Glory

For those who have been around Bethlehem Baptist Church for some time, you will know that our overwhelming spirit of worship and ministry and missions is aggressively proactive and positive. We do not define ourselves mainly by what we respond to or disagree with. But neither do we shrink back out of fear that others will define us this way.

The spirit of the church and the spirit of the school is the spirit of Christian Hedonism—in Jesus Christ, crucified and risen, God is 100 percent for us and not against us. "Christ also suffered once for sins, the righteous for the unrighteous, that he might bring us to God" (1 Pet. 3:18). And in bringing us to God, he brought us to our greatest Treasure and highest joy. To know him and enjoy him and show him in every way we can from his Word and his world is our passion, because we know that God is most glorified in us when we are most satisfied in him. When we rest in him as our supreme Treasure, especially in times of suffering, and continue to love others for his sake, we display the glory of Christ.

May God prosper this vision for the joy of all peoples and the glory of his Son.

Appendix 2

The Student, the Fish, and Agassiz

The first time I read this account of Agassiz and the fish was in the fall of 1968 during my first year in seminary. Daniel Fuller assigned it as part of his hermeneutics class. I was riveted. It came at a time when the particularities of the Bible were exploding with significance for me. I was seeing patterns and interrelationships and lines of thought that I had never seen before. And all of this was happening not because someone was telling me what to see, but because someone was telling me *look, look, look*.

I have taken this copy of "The Student, the Fish, and Agassiz" from David Howard's website and am including his introductory words, with his permission.[1] I have added this appendix because of how crucial it is that thinking deal with what is really there. We may be the most rational persons on the planet, but if our powers of observation are faulty, the intellectual houses we build may be built on sand. Here is Dr. Howard's introduction.

> The following is a classic account of the importance of firsthand observation, and careful, intense, focused study. It teaches lessons that apply to almost any discipline. Indeed, it is widely used in colleges and universities across the U.S. as a teaching tool in both the humanities and the sciences.
>
> Its lessons certainly apply to studying the Bible. Too often students of the Bible rely on secondhand, derivative knowledge acquired from pastors, teachers, parents, books about the Bible, or other secondary sources. While all of these have their place, there is no substitute, in the end, for one's own firsthand study and experience of the Scriptures, and for the joy of discovery.

---

[1]"The Student, the Fish, and Agassiz," http://www.bethel.edu/~dhoward/resources/Agassizfish/Agassizfish.htm.

The Student, the Fish, and Agassiz by the Student [Samuel H. Scudder][2]

It was more than fifteen years ago that I entered the laboratory of Professor Agassiz, and told him I had enrolled my name in the scientific school as a student of natural history. He asked me a few questions about my object in coming, my antecedents generally, the mode in which I afterwards proposed to use the knowledge I might acquire, and finally, whether I wished to study any special branch. To the latter I replied that while I wished to be well grounded in all departments of zoology, I purposed to devote myself specially to insects.

"When do you wish to begin?" he asked.

"Now," I replied.

This seemed to please him, and with an energetic "Very well," he reached from a shelf a huge jar of specimens in yellow alcohol.

"Take this fish," he said, "and look at it; we call it a Haemulon; by and by I will ask what you have seen."

With that he left me, but in a moment returned with explicit instructions as to the care of the object entrusted to me.

"No man is fit to be a naturalist," said he, "who does not know how to take care of specimens."

I was to keep the fish before me in a tin tray, and occasionally moisten the surface with alcohol from the jar, always taking care to replace the stopper tightly. Those were not the days of ground glass stoppers, and elegantly shaped exhibition jars; all the old students will recall the huge, neckless glass bottles with their leaky, wax-besmeared corks, half-eaten by insects and begrimed with cellar dust. Entomology was a cleaner science than ichthyology, but the example of the professor who had unhesitatingly plunged to the bottom of the jar to produce the fish was infectious; and though this alcohol had "a very ancient and fish-like smell," I really dared not show any aversion within these sacred precincts, and treated

---

the alcohol as though it were pure water. Still I was conscious of a passing feeling of disappointment, for gazing at a fish did not commend itself to an ardent entomologist. My friends at home, too, were annoyed, when they discovered that no amount of eau de cologne would drown the perfume which haunted me like a shadow.

In ten minutes I had seen all that could be seen in that fish, and started in search of the professor, who had, however, left the museum; and when I returned, after lingering over some of the odd animals stored in the upper apartment, my specimen was dry all over. I dashed the fluid over the fish as if to resuscitate it from a fainting-fit, and looked with anxiety for a return of a normal, sloppy appearance. This little excitement over, nothing was to be done but return to a steadfast gaze at my mute companion. Half an hour passed, an hour, another hour; the fish began to look loathsome. I turned it over and around; looked it in the face—ghastly; from behind, beneath, above, sideways, at a three-quarters view—just as ghastly. I was in despair; at an early hour, I concluded that lunch was necessary; so with infinite relief, the fish was carefully replaced in the jar, and for an hour I was free.

On my return, I learned that Professor Agassiz had been at the museum, but had gone and would not return for several hours. My fellow students were too busy to be disturbed by continued conversation. Slowly I drew forth that hideous fish, and with a feeling of desperation again looked at it. I might not use a magnifying glass; instruments of all kinds were interdicted. My two hands, my two eyes, and the fish; it seemed a most limited field. I pushed my fingers down its throat to see how sharp its teeth were. I began to count the scales in the different rows until I was convinced that that was nonsense. At last a happy thought struck me—I would draw the fish; and now with surprise I began to discover new features in the creature. Just then the professor returned.

"That is right," said he, "a pencil is one of the best eyes. I am glad to notice, too, that you keep your specimen wet and your bottle corked."

With these encouraging words he added—"Well, what is it like?"

He listened attentively to my brief rehearsal of the structure of parts whose names were still unknown to me; the fringed gill-arches and movable operculum; the pores of the head, fleshly lips, and lidless eyes; the lateral line, the spinous fin, and forked tail; the compressed and arched body. When I had finished, he waited as if expecting more, and then, with an air of disappointment: "You have not looked very carefully; why," he continued, more earnestly, "you haven't seen one of the most conspicuous features of the animal, which is as plainly before your eyes as the fish itself. Look again; look again!" And he left me to my misery.

I was piqued; I was mortified. Still more of that wretched fish? But now I set myself to the task with a will, and discovered one new thing after another, until I saw how just the professor's criticism had been. The afternoon passed quickly, and then, toward its close, the professor inquired,

"Do you see it yet?"

"No," I replied. "I am certain I do not, but I see how little I saw before."

"That is next best," said he earnestly, "but I won't hear you now; put away your fish and go home; perhaps you will be ready with a better answer in the morning. I will examine you before you look at the fish."

This was disconcerting; not only must I think of my fish all night, studying, without the object before me, what this unknown but most visible feature might be, but also, without reviewing my new discoveries, I must give an exact account of them the next day. I had a bad memory; so I walked home by Charles River in a distracted state, with my two perplexities.

The cordial greeting from the professor the next morning was reassuring; here was a man who seemed to be quite as anxious as I that I should see for myself what he saw.

"Do you perhaps mean," I asked, "that the fish has symmetrical sides with paired organs?"

His thoroughly pleased, "Of course, of course!" repaid the wakeful hours of the previous night. After he had discoursed most happily and enthusiastically—as he always did—upon the importance of this point, I ventured to ask what I should do next.

"Oh, look at your fish!" he said, and left me again to my own devices. In a little more than an hour he returned and heard my new catalogue.

"That is good, that is good!" he repeated, "but that is not all; go on." And so for three long days, he placed that fish before my eyes, forbidding me to look at anything else, or to use any artificial aid. "Look, look, look," was his repeated injunction.

This was the best entomological lesson I ever had—a lesson whose influence was extended to the details of every subsequent study; a legacy the professor has left to me, as he left it to many others, of inestimable value, which we could not buy, with which we cannot part.

A year afterwards, some of us were amusing ourselves with chalking outlandish beasts upon the blackboard. We drew prancing star-fishes; frogs in mortal combat; hydro-headed worms; stately craw-fishes, standing on their tails, bearing aloft umbrellas; and grotesque fishes, with gaping mouths and staring eyes. The professor came in shortly after, and was as much amused as any at our experiments. He looked at the fishes.

"Haemulons, every one of them," he said; "Mr. _____ drew them."

True; and to this day, if I attempt a fish, I can draw nothing but Haemulons.

The fourth day a second fish of the same group was placed beside the first, and I was bidden to point out the resemblances and differences between the two; another and another followed, until the entire family lay before me, and a whole legion of jars covered the table and surrounding shelves; the odor had become a pleasant perfume; and even now, the sight of an old six-inch worm-eaten cork brings fragrant memories!

The whole group of Haemulons was thus brought into review; and whether engaged upon the dissection of the internal organs, preparation and examination of the bony framework, or the description of the various parts, Agassiz's training in the method of observing facts in their orderly arrangement, was ever accompanied by the urgent exhortation not to be content with them.

"Facts are stupid things," he would say, "until brought into connection with some general law."

At the end of eight months, it was almost with reluctance that I left these friends and turned to insects; but what I gained by this outside experience has been of greater value than years of later investigation in my favorite groups.

Acknowledgments

The first two chapters of this book are a kind of "acknowledgments" for some of the key people and providences that put this book in motion—some of them years before there was any vision for writing at all. Which means that the all-foreknowing, all-planning God, as always, was at work and is the one we must always acknowledge above all. His creation of all things and sustaining of all things is supremely important. All else, and all others, are derivative.

Thank you, Noël and Talitha, for your support of my writing life. I take it less for granted now than I ever have. You have made so much possible without complaining. I love you.

Thank you, Bethlehem Baptist Church, and the Council of Elders in particular, for supporting me with yearly writing leaves that have made this book possible.

Thank you, David Mathis and Nathan Miller, for your partnership as assistants. You carry so much of my load and give so much help that I cannot see any book coming into existence without your help.

Thank you, Carol Steinbach, David Mathis, and the team for making the book more useful by providing the indexes.

And thank you, Lane Dennis, and the entire team at Crossway, who encourage me so much and provide such excellent workmanship and editing and support.

"The eye cannot say to the hand, 'I have no need of you.'" "For none of us lives to himself, and none of us dies to himself." I am happy to be a debtor to God's grace and a hundred acts of human love.

General Index

Scripture Index

✳ desiringGod

Everyone wants to be happy. Our website was born and built for happiness. We want people everywhere to understand and embrace the truth that *God is most glorified in us when we are most satisfied in him*. We've collected more than thirty years of John Piper's speaking and writing, including translations into more than forty languages. We also provide a daily stream of new written, audio, and video resources to help you find truth, purpose, and satisfaction that never end. And it's all available free of charge, thanks to the generosity of people who've been blessed by the ministry.

If you want more resources for true happiness, or if you want to learn more about our work at Desiring God, we invite you to visit us at www.desiringGod.org.